BOB RECCORD

FORGED BY FIRE

How God Shapes Those He Loves

Foreword by Bill Bright

BROADMAN & HOLMAN PUBLISHERS
Nashville, Tennessee

0-8054-2297-8

Published by Broadman & Holman Publishers,
Nashville, Tennessee

Dewey Decimal Classification: 248
Subject Heading: CHURCH \ CHRISTIAN LIFE
Library of Congress Card Catalog Number: 00-026681

Library of Congress Cataloging-in-Publication Data

Reccord, Robert E.
Forged by fire : how God shapes those He loves / Bob Reccord.
p. cm.
ISBN 0-8054-2297-8 (pb)
1. Christian life. [1. Joseph (Son of Jacob)] I. Title.
BV4501.2.R375 2000
248.4'861—dc21 00-026681
CIP

7 8 9 10 07 06 05 04 03

Foreword

FOR FORTY-NINE YEARS I HAVE TAUGHT, "GOD LOVES you and offers a wonderful plan for your life," the first law of our "Four Spiritual Laws" booklet that has been distributed to an estimated two billion people in every major language of the world. The biblical Joseph beautifully exemplifies this great truth and how it always proves true if we trust and obey.

I love Joseph, the son of Jacob, the son of Isaac, the son of Abraham. He is one of the most lovable and exemplary people of the Bible and one of my favorites. When I get to heaven, Joseph is one of the first people I want to meet! Sermons have been preached explaining the many ways in which Joseph's life paralleled that of our Lord Jesus Christ and how he was a prophetic type of Christ.

My beloved friend, Dr. Bob Reccord, gives us many wonderful insights into the life of this remarkable man and Bible hero, with a masterful job of helping us personally relate to him.

If you have ever been in what appeared to be a hopeless situation, or if you are now, you will be inspired by Joseph.

If you are presently in a place for which there seems no escape, this marvelous book will inspire you.

If you are uncertain and concerned about the future, Dr. Reccord's lessons from the life of Joseph will fill you with trust in the sovereignty and goodness of God. Joseph's total confidence in God and obedience to Him are great inspirations to me personally. They teach me that no matter what circumstances may be, if I trust in the Lord and obey Him, there will be eventual victory, and His promises will always be fulfilled in me.

Joseph was the epitome of God's instructions to us as recorded in Hebrews 10:35–36: "Do not throw away this confident trust in the Lord, no matter what happens. Remember the great reward it brings you! Patient endurance is what you need now, so you will continue to do God's will. Then you will receive all that he has promised" (NLT).

Dr. Reccord is one of the most knowledgeable and outstanding men of God I have ever known. I thank God for him, his great and influential ministry as president of the North American Mission Board, and for his marvelous work in putting together this inspirational and helpful book that will be a special blessing and inspiration to every reader.

Dr. Bill Bright
Founder and President,
Campus Crusade for Christ International

Table of Contents

ONE

Even the Little Flaws Matter

IT'S ONE OF THE MOST TRAGIC AIR DISASTERS of all time . . . and one of the most triumphant.

Captain Al Haynes lifted the United DC-10 into the air at Denver, Colorado, assuming it would be another routine flight. He had sat at controls for thirty-five years with United Airlines. Today United flight 232 would take him to a layover in Chicago and on to the final destination of Philadelphia.

At 2:09 P.M. on July 19, 1989, the wide-bodied jet lifted from the runway. The plane climbed and leveled off at a cruising altitude of 37,000 feet, with 295 passengers nestled into their seats. At 3:16 P.M. all hell literally broke loose, to quote many of the survivors.

The number-two engine, mounted high on the tail, suddenly made a resounding "boom," and the flight panel immediately showed that number-two engine had failed. Its hydraulic system had ceased to function. Frankly, that should be no difficulty for a DC-10. Three independent hydraulic systems build in what are called "redundancies." A complete hydraulic system can go down, and the plane will continue to fly, because the systems are completely self-sufficient. There's only one small area in the plane, a four-foot square toward the tail section, where all three redundant hydraulic systems converge. The odds of anything going wrong in that one small target area are *one billion to one*. But that day, the odds were apparently against the flight crew and the passengers.

Bill Records, the first officer, fought to control the plane, which had become *heavy* . . .

- No ailerons functioned—so the plane could not "bank."
- No rudders functioned—so the plane could not turn.
- No flaps on the leading edge worked—so the plane could not easily slow down except by throttle.
- No elevators worked—so the pitch of the airplane became very difficult to control.
- No flaps on the trailing edge worked—so landing looked to be almost an impossibility.
- No steering responded—so the plane would be out of control if they did manage to get the plane on the ground.
- No brakes worked—so if they got to the ground, how would they stop?

Captain Haynes and the crew concentrated on getting the plane to the ground with as few injuries as possible. While Haynes worked the vectors they would fly and kept communications with the tower and the passengers, Bill Records struggled to keep the plane in the air. Dudley Dvorak, the flight engineer, called United's San Francisco center, staffed around the clock with forty engineers to respond to emergencies. When he asked what was the standing operating procedure (SOP) for total hydraulic failure, there was sudden silence. The answer finally came back, "There is no SOP for total hydraulic failure, sir. It can't happen!"

As the plane became more and more difficult to handle, the crew found they could only turn to the right, and that only by varying the thrust of the two remaining engines. A DC-10 check pilot, who regularly flies with and checks out United's team of pilots, was sitting in the passenger section. Sensing something was dramatically wrong, he notified the crew that he was available if needed. Captain Haynes quickly brought Denny Fitch forward, and he began to help Records and Haynes control the throttles, and the resulting thrust, to begin a very delicate and difficult positioning to get the plane to the ground.

Unfortunately, the only airport the plane could approach was Sioux City, Iowa. Kevin Bockman, a twenty-seven-year-old control tower operator, found his hands full with a disaster waiting to happen. Ironically, he had just arrived in Sioux City, having been transferred from the East because he felt his previous assignment was "too stressful." He began a long and tedious communication process with Captain Haynes, doing everything he could to give courage for the difficult task at hand. One further complication: the Sioux City airport did not have a runway large enough for DC-10s. But that was their only choice.

As the plane lumbered in, crippled and wounded, the right wing touched the ground first. The plane cartwheeled and burst into fiery balls. That day, 187 lives were saved . . . 111 people died. The event may go down in history as one of the most heroic performances ever accomplished by any flight crew.[1]

What Caused the Crash?

Research by the National Transportation Safety Board (NTSB) indicated that a fan disk in engine number-two had exploded, and seventy pieces of shrapnel had ripped through the tail section of the plane, taking out the hydraulic system. The report traced the flawed engine fan disk all the way back to an ingot of titanium forged at Metals Corporation in Henderson, Nevada. Detailed records show it then went to ALCOA (Aluminum Company of America), where the six thousand-pound block of titanium was cut into eight sections and then crafted into high precision fan disks. Specifications for such high priority parts require incredibly detailed paper trails. When it was all said and done, the NTSB knew the exact segment of ore from which the defective fan disk came, even though eighteen years had elapsed from the raw material to the explosive blade.

Detailed investigation indicated that the forging process had not completely accomplished its goal. A small amount of nitrogen had not completely dissolved into the molten titanium. In its molten state, titanium can absorb small amounts of nitrogen, leaving microscopic vacuums which can become defects. The NTSB determined that the crack which caused the explosive tragedy occurred during the successive forging operations and heat treatment that formed the original part.

Forging is the metallurgical process by which molten metal is shaped and strengthened by hammering or pressure under heat. Most often forged metal is then placed in a die, or pushed or pulled through a die, so that the metal might attain its destined form for ultimate use. Most forging processes use extremely high heat and pressures that exert hundreds of tons of force. Presses used for forging parts for jet aircraft exert up to 50,000 tons of focused power to assure maximum efficiency for those parts.

In this particular case, the crack had developed very early in the life of the disk. It was exacerbated in the fatigue region with every take-off and landing cycle—15,503 of them in the life of that engine.

Even the Little Flaws Matter

None of us would get on an airplane that had a missing wing. It would be too noticeable. But how many of us would have thought about checking the stability of the fan disk in engine number-two? Yet, on that day in 1989, the fan disk was just as crucial as the wing to the plane's ability to fly.

Little flaws matter—and I don't mean just in metallurgy and aeronautics. I mean in life.

It seems at times that we have categorized sin as ranging from the "smallies" to the "biggies." People seem to feel they can make up their own list of what is a "smally" and what is a "biggy." Then they rationalize that if they just avoid the big ones and only trip over the small ones, everything will still be OK with God.

Nothing could be further from the truth.

In the Song of Solomon, God said it is often the little foxes that spoil the grapes on the vine (2:15). What did He mean? He was referring to the fact that you don't need a full-grown fox to ruin the grapes that hang low to the ground. Even the little ones can accomplish that. In my journey I've found it's usually the small things that make all the difference.

I heard about a pastor in a western city who went to the mall on a weekday to pick up a few things. As he walked through the mall, he noticed the music store was having a sale on CDs. A music lover, he veered into the store, found two CDs that he wanted, and headed toward the counter. He couldn't believe they were on sale—two for $9.99.

An outgoing person, he began to converse with those in line for the counter. When it came his turn, he simply handed a $50 bill to the girl at the counter, continued talking with those in line, grabbed his sack and change, and left. Not paying any attention, he just stuck the change in his pocket and finished his errands.

Getting into the car, he threw the sack into the front seat. It was then that the CDs spilled out, along with the receipt. As he placed them back into the sack, his eyes caught the fact that he had not been charged $9.99, but $1.99. Reaching into his pocket, he counted the change, and sure enough—he had too much.

He faced a dilemma, but following a few moments of inner conflict, he picked up the sack and marched back into the store. Waiting in line again, he finally came to the girl who had checked him out.

"I had to come back because you made a mistake," he reported. "Rather than charging me $9.99, you only charged me $1.99, and I didn't pay any attention to the change until I got to the car. I needed to come back and tell you."

Looking him straight in the eye, the clerk responded, "Oh, I didn't make a mistake. I knew exactly what I was doing. You see, I hadn't been in church for eighteen years, and on Sunday I decided to attend your church. You preached on integrity. When I saw you get in my line, I wanted to test you to see if you really live what you preach!" After an emotional pause, the pastor saw tears on the clerk's cheeks as she continued, "Mister, I don't know everything about this Christian faith stuff, but if Christ makes that kind of difference in your life, I need what you've got."

What if he had not paid attention to the little things? What if he had shown a "little flaw"? He would have "crashed and burned," at least in the eyes of one clerk at the music store. He would have said good-bye to a great opportunity to make a difference in someone's life. And very possibly the clerk could have been spiritually "critically injured" at best, or "fatally injured" at worst.

Forged by God's Fire

So, how does God shape us so we can detect and rectify even the small flaws? He uses the events of our lives to forge us into tools that are useful for building His kingdom. Just as critical parts for airplanes and other machines are shaped and strengthened by submitting them to heat and then hammering and pressing, often even forming them in a die, so God lovingly shapes, strengthens, and prepares each of us for ultimate use. He strives to remove even the smallest imperfections—even the ones that we've managed to hide from everyone else—because He knows they can surface at the most inopportune moments, wreaking havoc and disaster.

Throughout this book, we will see Him working in the life of the Old Testament character Joseph, to use his circumstances and shape him into a humble man of service. We'll also see how He wants to do that for each of us. You see, God wants to bring every individual to a designed end—that of intimate fellowship with Him through Jesus Christ His Son, *and* unselfish service to others.

Scripture describes God's goal so well when it says, "Consider it pure joy, my brothers, whenever you face trials of many kinds, because you know that the testing of your faith develops perseverance. Perseverance must finish its work so that you may be mature and complete, not lacking anything" (James 1:2–4).

With the importance of being forged in mind, you might find it intriguing to read that passage again. The word used for *face*, referring to our coming face-to-face with trials, literally means to "be surrounded as in a boxed canyon." The word for *trials* means "a trial or a testing directed toward a very specific end." The end toward which God directs our lives is that of being *mature*. This word in its original language refers to "having reached a designed end." That end is complete intimacy with God through Christ and complete usefulness in service to others.

But the process that gets us there requires perseverance, because we will be tempted to recoil from the heat of God's forging process or to lose sight of the finished end toward which He desires to take us. Knowing that very tendency, James went on to say, "If any of you lacks wisdom, he should ask God, who gives generously to all without finding fault, and it will be given to him. But when he asks, he must believe and not doubt, because he who doubts is like a wave of the sea, blown and tossed by the wind" (James 1:5–6).

God clearly says that if we can't understand the heat of His forging process while it is happening, we can ask Him to make clear what He is doing. He desires us to know His ultimate will for our lives, and it is always for our good.

God Has a Plan

Like the forger who understands the importance of extracting the metal from the ore, heating it into a molten substance, and then shaping it and increasing its strength by pressure and heat, God is busy attempting to make each of us into masterpieces He can use.[2] He reminds us of His intentions when He says, "'For I know the plans I have for you,' declares the LORD, 'plans to prosper you and not to harm you, plans to give you a hope and a future'" (Jer. 29:11).

For every individual, God has a very specific, original, and unique plan. He also has a plan for us to fit into His work corporately with others. And He begins that plan very early. The psalmist indicated that it actually begins before we are born (see Ps. 139).

So it was with Joseph in the Old Testament. From Joseph's beginning, God had a very special direction for his life. That direction would never take place in isolation but always in the context of family and community. And God did what He always does. He began with the end in mind. The psalmist summarized Joseph's experience like this:

> He [God] called down famine on the land
> and destroyed all their supplies of food;
> and he sent a man before them—
> Joseph, sold as a slave.
> They bruised his feet with shackles,
> his neck was put in irons,
> till what he foretold came to pass,
> till the word of the LORD proved him true.
> The king sent and released him,
> the ruler of peoples set him free.
> He [the king] made him master of his household,
> ruler over all he possessed,
> to instruct his princes as he [Joseph] pleased
> and teach his [the king's] elders wisdom.
>
> (Ps. 105:16–22)

With each step, God was forging Joseph to fulfill an ultimate end. And Joseph's life serves as an example of what He has in mind for all of us.

You see, God wants *you* to experience the ultimate fulfillment of walking in His will. He promises to help you overcome even the seemingly inexplicable challenges, hurts, disappointments, and adversities of life. And He will not keep His intentions secret forever. He has promised, "I will instruct you and teach you in the way you should go; / I will counsel you and watch over you" (Ps. 32:8). And He also declares, "Whether you turn to the right or to the left, your ears will hear a voice behind you, saying, 'This is the way; walk in it'" (Isa. 30:21). God is not in the business of playing hide-and-seek with His will. Rather, He is in the process of forging us into metal that can be used for His divine purposes.

God Provides a Process

Just as the process of forging is sequential and cumulative, so is the process of forging our lives through God's Word. Joseph would find that, as God was forging him into the character He could honor, the key was allowing God's Word to shape and refine his life. God's Word serves as a hammer and a fire in the forging process. While Joseph could only listen to God's spoken Word in his heart, we have the privilege of having access to God's written Word. And God clearly depicts what a powerful and productive tool it is in the forging process, refining us like fine metal and removing the dross of imperfections and vacuums from our lives.

> The law of the LORD is perfect,
>   reviving the soul.
> The statutes of the LORD are trustworthy,
>   making wise the simple.
> The precepts of the LORD are right,
>   giving joy to the heart.
> The commands of the LORD are radiant,
>   giving light to the eyes.
> The fear of the LORD is pure,
>   enduring forever.
> The ordinances of the LORD are sure
>   and altogether righteous.

They are more precious than gold,
than much pure gold;
they are sweeter than honey,
than honey from the comb.
By them is your servant warned;
in keeping them there is great reward.
(Ps. 19:7–11)

We Have a Choice

The one who forges our lives for unhindered intimacy with Him and unlimited service to others for Him is the one who also gives us the freedom to accept or reject His forging process. He is not a harsh and uncaring metalworker, but a loving and compassionate craftsman, attempting to shape our lives for maximum impact. But He will not force His work upon us, nor cram us into a die in which we are unwilling to be shaped. The choice is ours . . . that's one of the most amazing things about God. He gives you and me—and Joseph—freedom of choice. And that choice will make all the difference!

So I invite you to continue on the journey with me, to see how God forges a life for intimacy and impact, and how He strives to remove any impurities and vacuums that, with time, can cause stress fractures in life and bring about ultimate disaster.

Putting Yourself in the Refiner's Hands

1. Why do little flaws matter?
2. What is the process that removes flaws from metal when it is being formed into parts for machinery?
3. How does that reflect the process that God uses to remove flaws from our lives?

TWO

Heated to Create the Right Stuff

"FOR HE WILL BE LIKE A REFINER'S FIRE . . . HE will sit as a refiner and purifier of silver; . . . and refine them like gold and silver" (Mal. 3:2–3).

Imagine yourself in an ancient Judean village. The mid-afternoon sunlight filters through the dusty haze of a typical Middle Eastern day, and you stop to mop the perspiration from your face. You pause to rest in front of a small, shadow-filled structure. Peering inside, you see a man standing near the window. With callused but experienced hands, he holds what looks like a simple lump of rock. You see his silhouette, bathed in the sunshine streaming through his window. He takes that lump of rock and holds it up into the glinting streaks of natural light. And in that moment, the sun's rays dance off the flecks of metal, indicating veins of precious product hidden deep within the lump of ore.

With precisioned practice, despite the suffocating heat of the afternoon, this refiner starts a fire in the middle of the room. Using skills he learned at his father's side, he feeds air into the wood and watches the flames begin to dance. Heat begins to radiate from the center of the room, embracing everything in its path. Streams of perspiration spring from his concentrated face as the fire jitterbugs to the staccato rhythm of its own crackling. Waiting for it to achieve the proper temperature, the man turns to the side.

He picks up the lump of ore and places it in a rock bowl. Then he begins to hammer the lump. Cracking . . . chipping . . . breaking . . . pulverizing. The rock begins to crumble apart into a fine dust. Some might think he has ruined it. But he is actually embarking on a journey to maximize its potential.

The hammered bits of ore are dropped into a tempered crucible. The time is exactly right. The temperature has reached the strategic point. The ore begins to soften.

The silver or gold in the rock is of greater density and lower melting point than the limestone itself. It liquefies first. The sound of hissing and bubbling fills the room. The still solid impurities rise to the top. Carefully and slowly, the refiner skims aside the dross.

He returns the crucible to the center of the heat. Once again impurities rise, and once again he skims them away.

He throws small bits of charcoal into the molten liquid, not to darken it, but to enhance its sheen.

The novice may well think the process is all but complete. But the refiner knows better. He returns the crucible to the fire. As the heat caresses the tempered container, new impurities, heretofore unseen by the naked eye, float to the top. Once again, with pleased satisfaction, the man skims aside the slag.

He returns the crucible once again to the center of the fire. He watches. He waits. To the impatient observer, it seems tedious, tiresome, slow. But the refiner knows better. As the last flecks of dross float to the top, he skims the surface clean for the final time.

It's then that he begins to peer over the edge of the crucible. Slowly, expectantly he lowers the crucible away from the fire and moves his head in the proper position above it. And then it happens. It takes shape in a breathtaking moment. He sees an unmistakable reflection of his own face in the molten liquid. He knows the metal is ready . . . and he pours it into a mold.

Just as this Judean refiner purified the metal until he could see his face in it, so God, through Christ, desires to refine us until He sees His reflection in our lives. The mold into which He desires to pour the New Testament Christian is that of His own Son. His ultimate goal for each of us is that we would be "conformed to the image of His Son" (Rom. 8:29, NKJV). And like the skilled and ancient refiner, He will use a mixture of pressure, breaking, heat, and removing of impurities to bring us to the point where we are most useful.

So it was for Joseph in the Old Testament. His biography would compete with today's talk shows and soap operas. He faced a multitude of challenges, disappointments, heartbreaks, uncontrollable circumstances, unbelievable people, and inexplicable turns. But God used them to bring the heat that would produce the "right stuff" within him. He was:

- resented by many in his own family
- sold into slavery by his own brothers
- falsely accused of rape by his boss's wife
- unjustly thrown into prison to rot
- forgotten by the very people who could deliver him
- alienated from his family for years

Most of us will not face the challenges that Joseph did. And frankly, most of us will not ascend to his eventual level of authority and responsibility either. But God still has a plan for us—and it begins with His process to shape and mold us into people who reflect His character.

We'll look more carefully at Joseph's experience in later chapters. For now I'll just note that God assures us, as surely as He did Joseph, that "in all things God works for the good of those who love him, who have been called according to his purpose" (Rom. 8:28). But when you're walking through the heat, it's sometimes a challenge to keep that promise in focus. Yet all the while, the Divine Refiner is molding into your life and mine the very stuff needed for ultimate productivity . . . just like He did with Joseph.

The Bible records that when the heat of trials comes our way, God has a master plan in operation to give us "the right stuff." I find that Scripture repeatedly indicates six recurring themes that God creates in our lives by using trials. He taught them in Joseph's life, and He'll teach them in ours.

Clarifying God's Sovereignty

Either God is sovereign . . . or He's not.

The Holy Father wants us to live confidently with the assurance that He is in control in all that happens. From beginning to end, Scripture teaches that nothing happens in our lives unless it is first filtered through our loving Father's omnipotent hands.

Because of His sovereignty, God redeemed the multiplicity of challenging traumas through which Joseph passed, and He used them, not just for Joseph's ultimate good, but for the ultimate good of many others as well. God is not refining us so we alone might benefit from the results, but so that our lives might contribute significantly to those around us. Despite many frustrations, setbacks, disappointments, tragedies, and even betrayals, Joseph was still able to say to his brothers, "You intended to harm me, *but God intended it for good* to accomplish what is now being done, the saving of many lives" (Gen. 50:20, italics added). As we learn to view life through the lens of God's absolute control, we also learn to flex with any circumstance.

Unfortunately, some never come to that point—even some in religious leadership. Several years ago Rabbi Kushner wrote a book titled *When Bad Things Happen to Good People*. In it he said, "God wants the righteous to live peaceful, happy lives, *but sometimes even He can't bring it about*. It is too difficult even for God to keep cruelty and chaos from claiming their innocent victims" (italics added).[1] If indeed this perspective were to have validity, God basically becomes impotent. And besides, who would want to intimately know, follow, and trust a God who cannot control life in its totality?

This viewpoint inevitably grows from the habit of looking at life through a rational, reasoning lens rather than a lens of trusting faith. Instead, Joseph grasped that central truth that the church father Augustine would declare centuries later when he said, "Nothing, therefore, happens unless the Omnipotent wills it to happen; He either permits it to happen or brings it about Himself."

Like Joseph, the Old Testament character Job faced a series of fiery trials. Yet in the midst of his misery, Job understood that God's plan cannot be stopped, regardless of what people or circumstances may do. Boldly declaring his faith, he proclaimed, "I know that you [God] can do all things; / no plan of yours can be thwarted" (Job 42:2).

David also stated his confident trust in God's omnipotent sovereignty when he wrote, "He [God] will not let your foot slip— / he who watches over you will not slumber; / indeed, he who watches over Israel / will neither slumber nor sleep. / The LORD will keep you from all harm— / he will watch over your life; / the LORD will watch over your coming and going / both now and forevermore" (Ps. 121:3–4, 7–8).

Joseph, Job, and David all arrived at these conclusions because they saw God's hand delivering them from—but also refining them in—life's flaming adversities.

Testing Our Fidelity

In describing the forging process in our lives, Peter declared in the New Testament, "In this you greatly rejoice, though now for a little while you may have had to suffer grief in all kinds of trials. These have come so that your faith—of greater worth than gold, *which perishes even though refined by fire*—may be proved genuine and may result in praise, glory and honor when Jesus Christ is revealed" (1 Pet. 1:6–7, italics added).

Using the picture of refining precious metal, Peter explained what Joseph also knew—God allows trials into our lives so that our faith may be proved genuine, just like metal is tested for its purity. My friend, Adrian Rodgers, beautifully declared this principle in a sermon when he said, "The faith that cannot be tested is the faith that cannot be trusted."

God allows various trials to come to us so He can test the fidelity of our faith. In short, He wants us to answer a simple question—does our walk match our talk? In Deuteronomy 8,

God declared to Israel, "Remember how the LORD your God led you all the way in the desert these forty years, to humble you and to test you in order to know what was in your heart, whether or not you would keep his commands" (v. 2). Obviously God did not test the Israelites because *He* needed to know whether their faith was true. He already knew—He knows everything. Instead, He allowed the trials *so that Israel would know whether or not their faith was solid and deep.*

It is in the midst of adversity that we have the opportunity to bring honor and glory to God by trusting Him. And we can only do so as we answer three specific questions:

1. Can you trust God*?* Shadrach, Meshach, and Abednego reflected the same certainty that undergirded Joseph's ability to withstand incredible pressure. Facing the threat of being thrown into a furnace because they refused to worship any god other than the one true God, they proclaimed, "O Nebuchadnezzar, we do not need to defend ourselves before you in this matter. If we are thrown into the blazing furnace, the God we serve is able to save us from it, and he will rescue us from your hand, O king. But even if he does not, we want you to know, O king, that we will not serve your gods or worship the image of gold you have set up" (Dan. 3:16–18). Can you face any circumstance in life saying, "My God is able to deliver me . . . but even if He chooses not to, I will not stop trusting in Him"? Either God is sovereign, or He's not!

2. Can you trust *God?* Like Joseph, Job saw his life "going down the tubes" with calamity after calamity. Yet he stood firm and declared, "Though He [God] slay me, yet will I trust Him" (Job 13:15, NKJV). Regardless of the circumstance through which you are passing, or the disappointment from which you are reeling, can you put the full weight of your belief and trust on a God who promises to have everything in control?

3. Can you *trust God?* It always comes down to a personal decision. No one can make it for you. You have to exercise it yourself. Joseph would repeatedly be faced with circumstances that tested whether his walk of faith would match his talk of faith . . . and so will you and I.

Strengthening Our Dependency

Our heavenly Father wants us to know we can depend on Him without question or doubt. As we read through the Scriptures, we inevitably find three major principles:

1. God's love desires the best for us.
2. God's wisdom knows the best for us.
3. God's faithfulness accomplishes the best for us (whether it looks like it at the moment or not).

Repeatedly, when life seemed to be totally out of control, Joseph would have to depend on the fact that God knew what He was doing. In the New Testament, Paul would put it in his own words, ". . . We were under great pressure, far beyond our ability to endure, so that we despaired even of life. Indeed, in our hearts we felt the sentence of death. But this happened that we might not rely on ourselves but on God" (2 Cor. 1:8–9).

David, in one of his times of great difficulty and strife, said that his dependency on God resembled the way a frightened, running deer pants to be refreshed by streams of water. His own dependency on God was as total as the deer's upon the streams that gave it life. When challenges enclosed him, and he was tempted to strike out on his own independent course,

David's cry was this: "Why are you downcast, O my soul? / Why so disturbed within me? / Put your hope in God, / for I will yet praise him, / my Savior [Deliverer] and my God" (Ps. 42:11). Truly, adversity had taught him unconditional trust in God.

Removing Our Impurities

Through the course of his life, Joseph would learn a critical lesson: God was not nearly as interested in simply making him happy as He was in making him holy. Jerry Bridges, in his excellent book *Pursuit of Holiness*, records that the word *holy* is used over six hundred times in the Bible, as though God were trying to get a message across. He defines *holy* as "separated from sin and, therefore, consecrated to God." "The word signifies 'separation to God, and the conduct befitting those so separated.'"[2]

One of God's chief goals in the refining process of our lives is to allow the fires through which we pass to raise impurities to the top so they can be skimmed away. Just as the small nitrogen bubble in the fan disk of United Flight 232 caused a major catastrophe over time, God knows that even small weak points and impurities in our lives—given time—can bring major heartache.

Nor is God's call to a simple "cultural holiness." He is not looking for us simply to be nice people who comfortably fit in with all those around us. He is calling us to be a different people, with lives and character that reflect the countenance of the Refiner in our lives. We are not called to adapt to the culture in which we find ourselves, but instead to play a significant role in improving the culture in which we function.

We'll cover this in more depth later in the book. For now, let's just say that as holiness is forged into our lives, we are able to overcome the modern-day malady of AIDS. I'm not talking about the devastating disease known as Acquired Immune Deficiency Syndrome. Instead, I refer to perhaps an even greater threat of our day: Acquired *Integrity* Deficiency Syndrome. It occurs when the cracks of impurity lead us to compromise God's calling upon our lives.

How are you doing in the area of holiness? Joseph learned that even God's seemingly hard hand in our lives is for this very fact. The writer of Hebrews would put it this way, ". . . God disciplines us [through adversity] for our good, that we may share in his holiness" (Heb. 12:10). The amazing thing about holiness is that when we are holy according to God's Word, we will inevitably be happy.

Deepening Our Empathy

Ironically, it is often in life's deep valleys that we learn best how to minister to others. Everything that God allows in our lives prepares us to know Him more intimately and serve others more effectively. Each of Joseph's trials prepared him for the next touch he would give to another. Paul, in writing 2 Corinthians, summed it up well when he set forth this truth: "Praise be to the God and Father of our Lord Jesus Christ, the Father of compassion and the God of all comfort, who comforts us in all our troubles, so that we can comfort those in any trouble with the comfort we ourselves have received from God" (2 Cor. 1:3–4).

Early in our marriage, in an extremely demanding time in my ministry, Cheryl called me one day at the office. I was busily preparing for a major presentation at a national conference. When she said she needed to talk with me, I asked her to make it quick, for I was busy and focused. She hesitated quietly and then indicated she needed just a little more time than to simply be quick.

I then said, "OK, but if you can get to the bottom line as quickly as possible, it would help." (Of course, I said this very lovingly and tenderly!)

It was then that she unloaded the news that made my life stand still . . . the doctors had found a tumor in the pituitary area of her brain. Suddenly, things I had thought were critically important became almost insignificant.

As we walked through that difficult time, in which doctors told us we would probably never be able to have more children, we learned a number of things about God's faithfulness and sovereignty. And through that, we gained a great empathy toward others who are walking through deep valleys of crisis. Had we never gone through it, we would not have the empathy we do when someone says, "I'm really hurting." Are you walking through a fiery trial right now? Perhaps, as in Joseph's life, God is preparing you to minister to someone else. I know it's been true for me. And by the way . . . we had two more children! It's amazing how faithful God is, even in the deep valleys of trouble!

Developing Our Tenacity

As Joseph went through trial after trial, God was quietly developing a steel of endurance in him. In Hebrews 12 we are told that we are to run the race (life) that God has set before us with endurance (v. 1, NKJV). The word used in the Greek is *hupomone*. It does not simply refer to a "grin and bear it" attitude, or simply a "suck it up and get through it" declaration. Instead, it means "a confident and trusting, enduring constancy, even under a load of pressure." The ironic thing about life is that adversity produces endurance . . . and it's endurance that overcomes adversity.

After college and marriage, I found it easy to put on weight and get out of shape. A year ago, I became committed to working hard to take the "sag" out of my sagging waistline. Day after day, I worked hard on cardiovascular exercise and weight training, seeming to get nowhere. Straining. Sweating. Sucking wind. Questioning my sanity.

But then after several months, it was as though a quantum leap occurred. Weight began to drop off. Muscle began to get toned. And endurance increased significantly. Medical friends tell me that during the constancy of working out, regardless of how I felt, a whole new freeway system of small blood vessels and capillaries was forming within my body. Then came the day when they decided it was time for a "grand opening." Suddenly, more blood came flooding into the muscle tissue, and the resultant benefits seemed to be exponential.

Likewise, when we're walking through the depths of trials, God is building up a secondary support system of endurance, that we might be even more prepared for the next time adversity comes our way.

Why do I say "the next time"? Because just about everyone I meet is either coming out of some adversity, in the middle of some adversity, or getting ready to go into some adversity! God loves you too much to let you go through it alone.

The Right Stuff Makes All the Difference

As the refiner heats the metal to assure that the right qualities are in it, so God allows heat and pressure in our lives to enhance and deepen our strength and character. His ultimate goals are the strength of "spiritual metal" in our lives, and the usability of the end product in the lives of others.

Though it is not a picture of a refiner, but rather a weaver, this poem says it well in summary:

Life is a woven fabric;
  The pattern and web are wrought
By the dark threads and the golden
  That into the loom are shot.

You cannot judge God's purpose
  By the thrust of a single thread,
What to you may be dark, mysterious,
  May be gloriously bright instead.

For He holds in mind a pattern
  As fair as His love is strong,
Which grows each day in the weaving;
  Not a single thread goes wrong.

No warp in His hand shall tangle,
  No slumber His eyelids close;
We only can thwart His purpose
  When our stubborn wills impose.

Our tangled and broken efforts
  To walk in His kind commands
Will give life an added luster,
  Restored by His loving hands.

So trust in the Weaver's wisdom,
  In His love and unfailing care,
And the fabric of life, completed,
  Some day will be wondrous fair.[3]

Putting Yourself in the Refiner's Hands

1. Go back through the chapter and list the six major lessons that God teaches us through adversity.

2. According to what you have read in this chapter, define these terms:

   a. sovereignty—

   b. fidelity—

   c. dependency—

   d. impurities—

   e. empathy—

   f. tenacity—

3. How would you answer these questions?

   a. *Can you trust* God?

   b. *Can you* trust *God?*

   c. *Can* you *trust God?*

4. What are you facing right now that challenges your ability to answer those questions?

5. Write a simple prayer asking God to help you accept His sovereignty and learn His will through this experience.

THREE

Imperfections in the Base Metal

AS UNITED FLIGHT 232 ROSE THAT JULY DAY from Denver's airport and leveled off at 37,000 feet, everything appeared to be perfect and routine. All systems were "go." All mechanical functions were normal. Everybody in the cabin was comfortable.

Had anybody taken a look at the recorded history of engine number-two, they would have been more than confident of its stability. It was first installed on June 23, 1972, in the number-three position on a different United Airlines DC-10. There it accumulated over 40,000 hours of flying time and 16,139 cycles (takeoffs and landings).

The engine was then transferred to the number-one position on another United Airlines jet. Eight days later, for reasons of "convenience," engineers recorded that it was installed in the number-two position on the jet that would become United Airlines Flight 232. The installation date was October 25, 1988, and from that time, the engine had accumulated another 42,436 hours and 6,899 cycles (takeoffs and landings).

But, as investigation revealed following the tragic crash, the base metal flaw was there from the beginning. The small bubble of nitrogen in the molten titanium created a vacuum that was not filled, and it became the genesis of a structural fracture that would take down an entire wide-bodied jet.[1]

It Happens in Life Too

Several years ago, in a Virginia coastal town, a service man and his wife had three small children in stair-step succession. Only two years separated the three boys. The mother was elated, but the father was less than enamored. His favorite pastime was alcohol. And while some people are funny when they're drunk, he became more harsh and cruel.

Six months after the youngest child was born, the mother discovered she had cancer. Fight as she might, the combination of the demanding responsibilities with three toddlers and the heartbreaking reality of an alcoholic husband began to wear her down. Having fought for months, she finally gave out . . . and died.

The father now found himself responsible for not only a military career, but also for three small children. There were short periods when the boys seemed fun, but significant periods when they became a drain. The responsibility and demands were more than he wanted to face. Besides, the responsibilities got in the way of his enjoying alcohol. When he got tired of the boys, he would throw them out to another home, wherever they would be cared for. When he needed to feel good about himself, or to assure receipt of financial aid, he would grab them back.

The seemingly endless cycle occurred repeatedly until finally, having had all the fun he could stand, he threw them out for a final time. The boys were passed from hand to hand and from house to house, all the way from Virginia to southern Illinois, where they found themselves deposited temporarily in a home.

At the same time, a young couple in southern Illinois had attempted to have children and had seen four die during pregnancy or at birth. Hearing of these little fellows' plight, they found their way to the home and knocked on the front door.

"We understand you've got some little boys here who are in need of a home, and we thought we'd come and see if we could be of any help." The gruff lady at the door indicated that the two older boys had already been taken by a couple, but the "brat" was in the back.

Making their way through the house, they came to a back bedroom where the little guy was playing. It became obvious he had not been washed for days, and he sat in diapers that had long since needed changing . . . this despite the fact that he was well past diaper age.

What was worse, the little fellow was covered with a disease called impetigo. The disease creates sores throughout the body that weep and ooze with a pus-like substance. He was ghastly to look at.

Regardless, the young wife grabbed him up in her new dress and said, "We'll take him!" Leaving the home, they took him to a local doctor's office to have him examined. When the doctor entered the examining room and saw the child on the table, his first comment was, "My God! What do you want with that?"

Without hesitation, the young wife declared, "We're willing to take him, because if somebody like us doesn't, he'll never have the chance to become what God created him to be!"

How do I know this story so well? I was that little boy.

Imperfections in the Base Metal

The base metal of the circumstances of my life were anything but perfect. There were flaws at every turn. A dead natural mother. An alcoholic natural father. And even in the wonderful couple who adopted and raised me, the husband had grown up as a gang member and had always struggled with how to give and receive love.

Many of us find circumstances within our lives where the "base metal" of early occurrences is far from ideal. Imperfections can exist that, if not overcome, might later cause tragic dilemmas in life. And they come at us from various angles.

Taylor, for instance, grew up with an inaccurate view of God that formed a vacuum in the base metal of her life. She grew up in a home where her parents did not see God as a loving, caring Refiner with a wonderful plan. Instead they saw Him as a harsh and cruel taskmaster. She was taught that God was waiting to catch her making a mistake, and He would summarily *zap* her for her mistakes. As a result, her summarized biography looks more like a rap sheet.

- Age 7—began stealing from her mother's purse.
- Age 10—started smoking.
- Age 12—had her first sexual experience.
- Age 14—had become sexually active.
- Age 15—was an alcoholic.

In her late teen years, she went to Alcoholics Anonymous for help. She met some people she thought she could trust, but then three of those men gang-raped her. She then started doing drugs, which led her to turn her first "trick." From there she moved into prostitution. Having found life to be so empty in the war zone of prostitutes, she turned to lesbianism.

In the mire of that tragic and flawed journey, she heard a radio speaker say that God could forgive anything. That day she made a commitment to find a church and see if indeed that could be true. Arriving at a local congregation, hardened and embittered by life, with a countenance that reflected such hurt, she listened to a message of repentance, forgiveness, and God's plan for every life. That day, she committed to not staying a victim, but to becoming a victor through God's grace.

Or consider Gihwan (pronounced Kee-wan) Shin, who grew up with inadequate hope. Gihwan was born in Seoul, Korea. At the age of ten months, he became extremely ill, and the diagnosis was polio. As his young life unfolded, his mother told him this tragedy was punishment for the sins of his ancestors. He was offered no hope of ever getting any better. Growing up feeling ashamed, he hated his appearance, his life, and what he understood of God. He wanted to know why he deserved to be punished for what someone else did.

As a teenager, he stopped walking when he saw other kids. Wanting so badly to run and play with them, he was trapped in a body that had to drag a crippled leg. In his mind, the future looked hopeless, and no one told him any differently. Despair hung like a dense morning fog, blocking any sunlight of hope.

In 1974, at the age of 14, he had one of many surgeries to correct the residual damage left by the disease. While in the hospital, his cynical, bitter spirit was challenged when he saw other patients in even worse condition than himself. Patients with leprosy passed by with no fingers or hands, no toes or feet, and one without a nose. Yet something was different about them—they had smiles on their faces and seemed to have a song in their hearts. He couldn't understand what could make that kind of difference.

Into his room came a pastor who was also handicapped—suffering from blindness. Sensing Gihwan's bitterness, he simply explained how Jesus had made a difference in his life. As he shared the gospel, he read John 3:16, but the boy lashed back in anger and bitterness. The blind pastor simply said, "I cannot explain everything that happens, but I can explain that God loves you enough to change your life and give you hope."

Although the pastor left, his haunting words remained. His bottom-line message had been, "God loves you just the way you are, but He loves you far too much to let you stay there." In a short while, Gihwan opened his heart and invited Christ in with a simple prayer. Immediately, he began praying to see his family members come to know Christ as well.

In 1986, Gihwan came to the United States to continue his education in computer science. Through that journey, he sensed God's call into ministry and pursued the path of theological education. Today Gihwan serves in the state of Indiana as an Asian Catalytic Missionary for the North American Mission Board. He has personally started over twenty-five mission congregations and has personally introduced at least fifty people per year to a relationship with Jesus Christ in each of the last four years. In addition,

Gihwan's three sisters, one brother, and wife are now also Christians.

How easy it would have been for Gihwan to find himself trapped in the milieu of no hope and circumstances beyond his control . . . yet he became a victor.

A Crowd of Victims

Taylor or Gihwan could have easily succumbed to what our current culture calls "political correctness." A key ingredient of the "PC" atmosphere seems to be an unwillingness to take responsibility for one's own actions. The inevitable choice is to find someone to blame for difficulties. Fleeing from responsibility has almost become a national pastime.

In his book *A Nation of Victims*, Charles Sykes writes that two of the root causes seem to be an unhealthy self-centeredness and a relentless pursuit of an illusive quality called "happiness." De Tocqueville wrote years ago that he found Americans constantly brooding over things they did not possess rather than celebrating that which they had. He made himself a prophet, forecasting the arrival of the deadly and anesthetizing philosophy of victimization found so often in modernity.

Such a culture has led us to become a therapy-dependent continent. When difficulties come our way, we too often run to a psychotherapist who can help us explain away the problems by pointing a finger in some other direction. We blame inadequate parenting, unfortunate circumstances, less than ideal family life, an inability to practice our rights, too many restrictions, or some other—often nonsensical—dilemma.

Whatever happened to being responsible for our own decisions and for what we do with the cards we are dealt?

What If Joseph Had Lived Today?

If Joseph were in our society, he would have found it easy to point fingers at other people, making himself a victim of circumstance. Soap operas and bizarre stories told on TV talk shows have nothing on the story of Joseph's family. His father showed favoritism. His brothers were a rebellious, jealous lot. His mother was over-protective.

Reuben, the oldest brother, was disinherited because he slept with his father's concubine. Dinah, the daughter, was raped by the son of the town mayor. Then Simeon and Levi, along with their brothers, plotted revenge for Dinah, deceived the young men of the community, and slaughtered them all. If you haven't yet had your fill of sordidness, consider Joseph's brother Judah. Thinking he had sneaked out to have sex with a prostitute, he discovered he had been sleeping with his daughter-in-law.

That gives you a picture of Joseph's "happy little family." He had weak, ineffective parents and was surrounded by jealous and vicious siblings. It may sound like an ideal scenario for a TV soap opera, but it's not the best kind of setting in which to be raised. Still, that's where God placed Joseph.

And with that background, Joseph could have developed a victim mentality. Instead, he chose to become a victor. He somehow came to understand that *he alone* was responsible for his own decisions. Only he could determine whether to try to swallow lemons or to create lemonade from the circumstances in which his life was launched. So it is with us. Our decisions determine our destinies. While God may orchestrate our circumstances, he allows us alone the freedom to respond to them. The difficult ones either will be seen as stumbling blocks or as stepping stones . . . but the choice is ours.

And let's face it, all of us can find some defective base-metal circumstances from our early lives to blame if we so choose. All we have to do is look hard enough.

Overcoming Defective Starts

So how do we overcome a difficult beginning in life? How do we make choices that make us victors rather than victims? Let me offer a few suggestions.

1. *Acknowledge God's sovereignty.* As we get further into this book and cover the details of Joseph's life, you will find that the overwhelming theme of his biography is the simple reality that God is always in control of everything. Perhaps the clearest indication of that occurs near the end of his story, when Joseph clearly tells his brothers, "You intended to harm me, but God intended it for good . . ." (Gen. 50:20). He understood that every circumstance of his life happened with either the initiation or the permission of a loving God. If he looked for someone to blame, then he ultimately would have to point far enough to reach all the way to God. The same is true for you and me.

2. *Beware the therapeutic trap.* The tragic error of a therapy-driven culture is the removal of a sense of sin. It is replaced by blame. In his book *The Shrinking of America*, Dr. Bernie Zilbergelt declares, "In the therapeutic view, people are not regarded as vile or as having done anything they should feel guilty about, but there is certainly something wrong with them. Specifically, they are too guilty, too inhibited, not confident and assertive enough, not able to express and fulfill themselves properly, and without a doubt, not as

joyful and as free from stress as they ought to be."[2] As a result, the question captured by the book several years ago by Dr. Karl Menninger, *Whatever Became of Sin?*, becomes critically relevant. The author notes that sin is replaced by social phobias, fears, and by a battle cry of "I deserve to be happy."

3. Choose responsibility. Victor Frankl, who was humiliated, tortured, and dehumanized in Nazi prison camps, declared, "The last of all great human freedoms is to choose one's response in any given set of circumstances."[3] Taking responsibility is a choice . . . albeit not always an easy or comfortable one. But the choice is essential in living life to the fullest and becoming a mature, responsible, and balanced adult. Only you can decide to "step up to the plate."

4. Avoid the lure of immediate gratification. Our society is driven by the belief that gratification is a right and one which is deserved immediately. We'll talk about this more later, but for now let's just say that Joseph certainly had opportunity to give in to this lure when his boss's wife tried to seduce him. He could have chosen to point his finger when false accusations sent him to prison. And finally, when he had risen to the office of prime minister of all Egypt, he could have exacted revenge on his family. Instead, he chose to serve God rather than his own appetites.

5. Cultivate a spontaneous obedience. Joseph's attitude of respectful obedience is reflected in Genesis 37, when his father asked him to check on his brothers—the same brothers who were constantly degrading him. Joseph didn't even hesitate. He responded immediately, unquestioningly. This attitude would be reflected throughout Joseph's life, not only to his family, but also to his God. When God indicated a direction Joseph was to take, he followed it with diligence.

The German theologian and martyr Dietrich Bonhoeffer poignantly stated the importance of this kind of obedience when he wrote, "Only he who believes is obedient, and only he who is obedient believes."[4] His sentiment echoes that which Jesus expressed in the closing illustration of his Sermon on the Mount. He drew an analogy between a man who is obedient and one who builds his house on a very solid foundation. When the rains of adversity fall and the streams of disillusionment and discouragement arise, and the prevailing winds of pain and difficulty blow, the house stands firm. Jesus declared that our lives will do the same if we obey His Word.

6. Cultivate an attitude that sees the glass as "half full" rather than "half empty." Despite the fact that his brothers berated him and were vicious in their jealousy, Joseph chose to look at life through a positive lens. He knew that God had something in store for him, regardless of his background. He attempted to translate that belief to his brothers, though it was interpreted by them as sheer arrogance. Regardless, Joseph anchored his attitude in a true understanding of God's promise to him. He refused to let go of that promise, and his resulting attitude allowed him to hurdle great difficulty. He refused to succumb to unexpected and unpleasant circumstances.

One of my favorite stories is about two hunting buddies. One of them always saw things from a positive perspective. The other was never positive about anything. Tired of his friend's negative attitude, the positive sportsman decided to try to change his hunting companion's attitude.

With this goal in mind, he purchased the finest hunting dog he could afford. As duck season approached, he taught his dog to retrieve the ducks. His method of teaching, however, differed radically from the norm. Rather than teaching the dog to swim, he taught the dog to walk on water.

On the opening morning of duck season, the positive hunter picked up his negative partner and headed for the lake. Once situated in their blind, their decoys positioned in the water around them, the positive hunter began his familiar and famous duck call. Soon several ducks flew in low. The hunters opened fire and ducks began to fall from the sky. The moment of truth had arrived!

At the appropriate command, the new dog leaped out of the blind and stepped across the water to the downed ducks. He picked up the game and brought them back to the blind. With pride and amusement on his face, the joyful, positive hunter looked at his friend and asked, "How do you like that?"

The negative hunter grunted in reply, "I see you got stuck with a dog that can't swim."

During your lifetime you will probably encounter many people who see life through the same lens as the negative hunter. Just remember that the person who overcomes the odds in life will be the victor rather than the victim. His or her motto will be, "Keep your chin up and your knees down."

Thus it is that even a defect in the base metal of the early circumstances of our lives can be detected and corrected if we'll just be diligent in our responsibility.

Putting Yourself in the Refiner's Hands

1. Describe some of the "cracks" in your own base metal.

2. List the six steps to overcoming defective starts.
3. Use this scale to fill in numbers that best represent how your life presently reflects the following qualities: 0 = none at all; 1 = not much; 2 = somewhat; 3 = on and off; 4 = positively growing; 5 = practicing regularly.

_____ God is in control of every circumstance in my life.

_____ I am responsible for choosing my response to every situation in my life.

_____ I can either serve God, or I can serve my own desires, but I can't serve both.

_____ The person who loves God seeks also to obey Him.

_____ A positive mental attitude is possible, regardless of the circumstances in which I find myself, when it is anchored in a true understanding that God has a plan for me, and it is for my benefit.

4. Rate yourself on this continuum:

Victim Victor

0 1 2 3 4 5 6 7 8 9 10

F O U R

Heat from Unexpected Sources

I REMEMBER WHEN WE WERE EXPECTING OUR second child. Christy, our oldest, had ruled the roost for three and a half years. Her private domain was about to be invaded by a newcomer.

Cheryl delivered our second, Bryan, at the appropriate time, and everything went fine. As the day approached to bring Bryan home, Christy developed a cold. We explained to her that we must be very careful with the new baby and make sure he was not infected with her germs. Otherwise he would have to go back to the hospital.

As the initial days crept by, Christy's cough hung on. So did her feeling that her domain had been invaded. As Cheryl was walking down the hall toward another room, she heard a strange sound emanating from where Bryan was sleeping. Peering around the door, she found Christy standing on a chair, hunched over Bryan's bassinet, coughing with everything she had. Evidently, she figured that if she could just spread some germs, she could send one baby brother back to the hospital and out of her kingdom.

Sometimes our greatest challenges come from unexpected places. Fellow Christians. Coworkers. Church staff. Friends. Family members. And best friends.

The Refining Process

One of the keys in forging and refining is the constancy of the heat. If heat comes rushing from unexpected sources, explosions can occur. So in life, heat can come from unexpected directions, and it can produce potential explosions if we don't respond correctly.

As we saw in the previous chapter, the cards were stacked against Joseph. His home life was anything but peaceful. His brothers were violent, headstrong young men. They lacked any understanding of or submission to moral boundaries. His sister had been violated. And his father's naiveté and favoritism had, perhaps, been the fatal blow to Joseph's relationships with his siblings.

Despite growing up in this unstable environment, Joseph possessed a sense of destiny, undergirded by two God-given dreams giving glimpses into his future.

Joseph was a "dreamer"

Genesis 37:5–11 recounts Joseph's dreams, as he described them to his brothers. They were all together, working in the fields and "binding sheaves of grain." Suddenly, Joseph said, his bundle rose and stood above the rest. This seemed to predict that his brothers would eventually bow before him.

You can imagine their response. It would be an understatement to say they weren't happy with Joseph's dream or its obvious meaning.

"Do you intend to reign over us? Will you actually rule us?" (Gen. 37:8) they asked. Joseph stood there in his multicolored robe—a gift from his father symbolizing the preferential treatment which ripped apart this family—and he basically told them that one day he would be head honcho. Their verbal response was one of total incredulity, and it was backed up by an emotional reaction: "And they hated him all the more because of his dream and what he had said" (Gen. 37:8).

Not content, Joseph twisted the proverbial knife by proceeding to tell them of a second dream, in which the sun and moon and eleven stars bowed down to him (Gen. 37:9). If he had left any doubt in reporting the first dream, his message was clear in the second. The stars referred to the brothers. The temperature began to rise dramatically—the brothers were getting hotter by the moment.

Scripture doesn't clearly explain why Joseph shared these dreams with his brothers. Perhaps he was just caught up in the moment and couldn't help repeating what he had experienced. Perhaps he was awkwardly trying to gain his brothers' acceptance and encouragement. Perhaps he was so used to favoritism that it never crossed his mind how his brothers would react. Maybe the fact that he was seventeen is explanation enough.

We don't know his motivations, but we do know his brothers grew angrier and more frustrated. We can assume they talked to one another, fueling their hatred until it raged out of control. For days, and possibly months, the brothers fumed over the preposterous dreams that Joseph had shared with them. Over their dead bodies would he become their superior. One way or the other they would find a way to stop him.

Joseph's Brothers Take Revenge

Their time finally came when Jacob sent Joseph to see how his brothers were doing as they tended sheep. Scripture tells of their reaction upon seeing him coming: "Here comes that dreamer! . . . Come now, let's kill him and throw him into one of these cisterns and say that a ferocious animal devoured him. Then we'll see what comes of his dreams" (Gen. 37:19–20).

The die was cast. Their abrasive natures, probably multiplied by the group mentality, determined to wreak vengeance, not just on Joseph, but also on their father. They would strike at the very heart of everything they saw to be unfair in their lives.

But Reuben, the oldest brother, had more maturity and common sense than the others. He set forth the idea of throwing this young upstart in the cistern—so Joseph was literally in a pit. To cover up their deed, Joseph's brothers stripped off his robe—the one his father had given him—and blotted it with animal blood. They would then tell their father that the young brother had been killed. What an excellent cover-up! Sometimes fire comes from the strangest places!

What Brings on Such Adverse Reactions?

We've already looked at some of the factors that placed Joseph right in the center of a family furnace. They are, of course, the same factors that often put us in adverse circumstances, and they are especially evident when other people are involved in that process—even if it's just a figurative pit of failure, depression, fear, rage, or some other agony.

You can read with regularity in newspapers of families torn apart by underlying currents of uncontrolled emotion.

How they respond is sometimes more difficult to believe than the wildest fiction. If you doubt that, just watch the Jerry Springer Show or Sally Jesse Raphael.

Joseph's story is no exception. It clearly describes the lack of boundaries controlling behavior when men and women ignore their God-given consciences and ascribe to a lifestyle that allows for the sinful nature to take control. Certainly their reaction to Joseph underscores man's propensity for evil.

Throughout history many people have excused their own sins in the name of "vengeance." Joseph's brothers were no different, and unfortunately, neither are you or I. You see, it's pretty easy to stoke fires of hatred in anyone who thinks he or she has been wronged. Emotions, obviously, fuel fires in the context of human relationships. They can cause what began as a tiny spark to burst into a raging flame. The heat from the ensuing emotional inferno can severely burn everyone involved.

Emotional Matchsticks

Take a look at some of these emotional matchsticks that led to Joseph's seeming demise at such a tender age:

1. Jealousy. "When his brothers saw that their father loved him more than any of them, they hated him and could not speak a kind word to him" (Gen. 37:4). Webster's Dictionary defines *jealous* as being "intolerant of rivalry . . . apprehensive of the loss of another's exclusive devotion; hostile toward a rival or one believed to enjoy an advantage." Jacob inadvertently struck the match of jealousy when he clearly demonstrated that Joseph was his favorite son.

2. Envy. Webster describes envy as one step past jealousy. It is the "painful or resentful awareness of an advantage enjoyed by another joined with a desire to possess the same." Joseph's brothers envied his special attention. Why didn't they all have gorgeous robes? Why did they have to work hard while he supervised? The questions were innumerable, and as they continually went unanswered, their envy reached the point where they were ready to commit murder in order to get rid of the one who had what they wanted—their father's acceptance and approval.

It may be true that, if Joseph had behaved differently, he could have quelled some of these reactions. Scripture doesn't indicate much effort on his part to do so. Still, most of Joseph's actions probably were inadvertent. He had never been anything but the favorite, so he had nothing to compare with his own experience. And as we noted, he was a mere teenager. I don't know about you, but I didn't show a lot of relational wisdom in my teen years. It's entirely possible that he didn't mean to stir up envy—he just didn't think about it at all. Or he simply didn't know what to do about it.

Meanwhile, the ravenous appetite of envy was eating at his brothers' hearts. They were literally sick with their desire to be in his shoes. Scripture tells us, "A heart at peace gives life to the body, / but envy rots the bones" (Prov. 14:30).

3. Bitterness. Jealousy and envy eventually evolved into full-blown bitterness for Joseph's brothers. Scripture warns us all of the deadly effect of this emotional stronghold.[1] The actions and reactions of Joseph's brothers give a clear picture of what happens to an individual struggling with bitterness. This person will waste excessive amounts of emotional energy in self-pity or in planning revenge. He won't enjoy present circumstances because he is bound up in negativity. His perspective is clouded. His relationships are scarred. He nurtures bitterness until it becomes a poisonous influence on all with whom he associates.

Then add this kind of fuel to the fire: personality conflict, fear of or resistance to change, unmet expectations, and the threat of losing control. Suddenly circumstances can get volatile. In families. Around churches. Among friends. Within ministries. At businesses. The fire of adversity can rage . . . even from the most unexpected directions. Just like in the metal refining process, unexpected hot flashes can spell disaster . . . unless they are controlled and managed.

Joseph found this to be true in his own family. And then, sitting in the pit, he had to come to grips with his circumstances. He had a choice. He could allow his brothers' abrasiveness and bitterness to control his life—seeking his own vengeance or succumbing to a victim mentality. Or he could allow God to use the negative consequences of family infighting as a crucible to mold and purify his own character.

Principles for Dealing with Adverse Circumstances

Certainly, according to human thinking, Joseph would have been perfectly within his rights to surrender to a harsh attitude as he sat in that pit. This attitude is captured in the bumper sticker that reads, "Don't get mad—get even!" Most of us would also understand if he simply gave up, succumbing to the negative emotions of doubt and fear and even inward anger. Friedrich Nietzsche called revenge "the greatest instinct of the human race."

Imagine yourself in Joseph's place—he was in the middle of nowhere and had no help. There was no way out. And worse, no one cared—maybe not even God. "If He cares, why doesn't He get me out of this mess?" Surely such thoughts taunted Joseph, simply because of his humanity.

But God did care! Acts 7:9 tells us, "Because the patriarchs were jealous of Joseph, they sold him as a slave into Egypt. But God was with him . . ." *But God*—those two words completely revolutionize any circumstance. And those two words can raise us from tragedy to triumph in any situation.

You see, it's always too soon to throw in the towel. Real courage is the ability to endure five minutes more. Joseph couldn't afford to give up. It has been said that the measure of a man is found in what it takes to make him quit.

Winston Churchill was such a man. While young, he attended a preparatory school by the name of Harrow. Following his time there, he completed his education and served in the military in both India and Africa. At the age of sixty-five, this five-foot, five-inch tall giant was elected as prime minister of England.

Toward the end of his career he was invited to address the student body at his alma mater. The day preceding his arrival, the headmaster announced, "I would encourage you to bring pen and paper tomorrow. The prime minister will speak and you will wish to note his comments. He is possibly the greatest orator of all time."

The following day the auditorium was packed and each pen hoisted. After a rather effusive introduction, Mr. Churchill stepped to the podium. Graciously he acknowledged all. Then in his powerfully authoritative voice, he rumbled: "Never give up. Never give up. Never give up. Never! NEVER!"

With that, he sat down.

So it was with Joseph—and it should be with us. It's always too soon to give up.

Paul teaches us this in Philippians 3:13–14: "Forgetting what is behind and straining toward what is ahead . . . press on toward the goal to win the prize for which God has called me [us] heavenward in Christ Jesus." He had been stoned in Lystra. Fomented riots in Ephesus. Received threats in Corinth. Was shipwrecked in Malta. And now he was probably writing this from a Roman prison as he neared the end of his life. Yet even here he could not give up. He realized that the key was forgetting the circumstances of the past. The goal at that point was to press toward the future and to make his life count where he was.

In the same manner, Joseph would have to forget the adverse circumstances of the past, putting them forever behind him. He couldn't dwell on the favoritism shown by his father. And he would have to move beyond the jealousy, envy, and bitterness shown by his brothers.

When mistreated, our most natural instinct is to choose either hurtful words and actions to retaliate, or to pull within ourselves in anger, waiting for an opportunity to deal out manipulative revenge. Yet Scripture says something far different. First Peter 2:19–20 tells us, "It is commendable if a man bears up under the pain of unjust suffering because he is conscious of God . . . if you suffer for doing good and you endure it, this is commendable before God." This type of biblical attitude neutralizes the attitude of getting even. It is a healing choice to be aggressive in forgiving and forgetting rather than in retaliating. But it is so hard to do until we feel the score has been settled.

When unexpected heat comes from relationships, we must make some very critical choices. You may have grown up in a home where conflict was the norm. You may believe that fighting it out is the normal way to deal with conflict. On the other hand, you may have come from a home where hurt from close relationships was suppressed and never expressed. As a result, people in your family swept honesty under the carpet and played cruel, manipulative games with one another. In either case, your choice between "fight" or "flight" left you with a choice between two forms of disaster.

When conflict comes from unexpected sources, God's principle is to focus not on winning or losing but on healing the conflict at hand. It is the call of God to surrender your rights in order to do whatever it takes to salvage both the relationship and your own integrity.

Several years ago, in his book *The Healing Choice*, Ron Lee Davis explained, "The healing of our relationships and our conflicts begins when we stop saying, 'Yes, but—' and start simply saying *Yes*; when we stop defending ourselves and blaming others, and begin taking ownership of our own failures and sins; when we recognize that our attitude is always ours to choose. The healing choice in a time of conflict is the decision to stop saying, '*You* make me angry,' and to start saying, '*I'm* feeling angry about the problem between us.' Let's focus our energy on solving the problem, not on hurting each other."[2]

If we truly intend to honor God, and in the process, to gain some measure of emotional and spiritual health, we must not settle for "keeping on keeping on." It's simply not enough. We must keep on with the right attitude and focus. Our pressing on must be with the goal of recovering from and overcoming the adversities. We must not abandon the desire to make a meaningful contribution in and to the lives of those around us. It's never too late to get a fresh start.

One last principle I've learned applies when the fires of adversity come from seemingly friendly forces. Hard-knock experience has taught me to listen carefully to what's being said. Even if ninety percent is incorrect, but ten percent has a grain of truth, I need to grab hold of that grain. Inevitably, I have found there is most often a kernel of truth I need to hear when the fire of adversity comes from seemingly friendly forces. That ten percent of truth may help me salvage a relationship, smooth a misunderstanding, overcome an inequity, correct a mistake, or strengthen a weakness. We are never so right that we cannot learn where we may be wrong.

Could it be that, during the times of isolation, Joseph realized that the attitude with which he had shared his early dreams among his family may have had an edge of cockiness or arrogance—even if the cause was nothing more than his youthful naiveté?

Promise in the Midst of Adverse Circumstances

Situations are not always as they seem on the surface. Had Joseph looked around the walls of the pit and taken things at face value, he would have determined that his life, for all practical purposes, was over. The God in whom he had trusted would have seemed untrustworthy. The dream of the future would have turned to a living nightmare.

But God tells us not to look merely at outward circumstances. Nor are we to merely evaluate things from our perspective. God tells us, "Trust in the LORD with all your heart / and lean not on your own understanding; / in all your ways acknowledge him, / and he will make your paths straight" (Prov. 3:5–6). He doesn't tell us not to use our understanding. Instead, He tells us not to trust totally in our own thought processes. This is because our understanding is usually limited in perspective. It sees only the obvious, and its knowledge is limited to the present and the past. Behind seemingly adverse circumstances, God may well be at work making the pathway of our life travel in the direction He desires.

You see, when someone else's jealousy or envy or bitterness pushes us into a searing furnace, God is still working out His plan. Usually He is preparing us for something better than we ever imagined—but we'd never be able to handle it if it weren't for what we learn while we're facing the fire.

In Romans 8:28, the apostle Paul explained this process: "We know that in all things God works for the good of those who love him, who have been called according to his purpose." He elaborates that purpose in verse 29 when he says we are ". . . to be conformed to the likeness of his Son . . ." That means God is concerned about who I am—from the inside out. He wants me to be like Jesus. And He's so intent on that, He will work in the circumstances of my life to bring about that result.

God doesn't say that everything that happens to us is necessarily good. He, instead, says that "in all things God works for the good."

Certainly, Joseph's experience is a perfect example. God used his brothers' lack of character to mold Joseph into a man of character—a man who thought and said and did what Jesus would do in the same situation.

Often in life's hardships, we'd like to skip the battle and go right to the victory celebration. That's not God's plan. Through all of our experiences, God works to broaden our capacities and abilities. He fine-tunes our character. God takes us through a spiritual expansion program to enlarge us so we can enjoy greater spiritual growth and manifold blessings. Often, he uses other people as hammers and presses, tempering and shaping the metal of our lives. This process doesn't happen overnight. In fact, shortcuts can be devastating.

God's promise in Isaiah 43 has taken me through so many unexpected fires. There He proclaims, "But now, this is what the LORD says— / he who created you, O Jacob, / he who formed you, O Israel: / 'Fear not, for I have redeemed you; / I have summoned you by name; / you are mine . . . / When you walk through the fire, / you will not be burned; / the flames will not set you ablaze'" (vv. 1–2).

Isn't it interesting that the idioms Isaiah used in declaring God's promise are idioms we still use today. The water's getting deep. The currents are moving fast. The fire is getting hot. I'm going to get burned in this situation. As His promise was to Israel through Isaiah, so it is to us today. God doesn't ever forget to honor His Word.

God's Forging Process

If we are to possess the character qualities that undergird spiritual perseverance over an entire lifetime, we must submit to God's forging process. His most effective tool is adversity. Some things that occur in our lives won't be pleasant. We must trust God's plan, knowing that He wants our best and accepting that the best isn't always the easiest.

Several years ago, I was water skiing with a large group of young people. While I was slalom skiing, the tip of my ski caught a wake and turned me into a human cartwheel. Upon surfacing and feeling a strange sensation in my left leg, I found that my foot was pointed 180 degrees in the wrong direction. Twisting it around to its correct position, I told no one of the injury. After all, we were there to have a good time.

Five days later, when I could no longer stand the pain, I went to the hospital emergency room. An orthopedic surgeon was immediately called and, upon checking x-rays, he found that I had torn major ligaments and cartilage in the leg.

To this day I recall the excruciatingly painful work done on my knee. This was followed by four months in a cast from my hip to my ankle. Then came the real affliction—several weeks of nerve-shattering exercises to strengthen the leg back to its normal health. Though the medical treatment was best for me in the long run, it was extremely painful in the short run.

We don't have to travel through many years as Christians to be able to look back on things that seemed disastrous at the time, but which have turned out to work for our good. Disappointments have turned into blessings. In the midst of struggles, we can see in hindsight that a guiding hand directed us through life's maze. In all of it, God has hammered out the character He desires in our lives on the anvil of experience and trial.

So be assured that even when you're in a pit, God hears your cry for help. "The righteous cry out, and the LORD hears them; / he delivers them from all their troubles" (Ps. 34:17).

The Purpose of the Furnace

God had a purpose for Joseph's experience in the fiery furnace of family relationships. And He has reasons for the flames you have endured as well. God uses such dilemmas to work out His divine purpose in our lives. God was hammering out the metal in Joseph's life that only He knew the young man would need. We later find Him doing the same thing with Israel.

During the 40 years that Israel spent wandering in the wilderness, God was forging a people who would obediently endure and persevere to the point of victory. In Deuteronomy 8:2 we read: "Remember how the LORD your God led you all the way in the desert these forty years, to humble you and to test you in order to know what was in your heart, whether or not you would keep his commands."

God is in the process of showing us our inability to handle life without depending on Him. Humility comes in realizing that we are not as self-sufficient as we think. Sometimes God is forced to allow us to endure trial, because it's the only way He can get our attention. Unfortunately, even there, much too often we are looking for an easy way out or still attempting to accomplish our own self-centered purposes.

A story is told of a young man walking along a mountain path watching the sun set. Captivated by the splendor of color on the horizon, he slipped over the edge and tumbled over the sheer precipice.

The drop was a thousand feet to the canyon floor. Five hundred feet down the sheer face of the cliff, the young man caught himself on a jutting limb. Hanging desperately in midair, he yelled out into the vast expanse of space, "Is anybody out there?"

Remarkably, a deep, resonant voice responded, "Yes, my son, I am here."

The young man yelled back, "Get me out of here!"

Again, the resonant voice came: "Do you totally trust me?"

Getting impatient, the young man yelled, "Of course, I trust you. Get me out of here!"

"If you trust me, LET GO."

Suspended in time and space, the young man hung there momentarily, then shouted, "Is anybody else out there?"

In our dealings with God, have we responded much differently than that young man? God allows us to be tested to bring us to the end of ourselves. He then tests us to see what is really in our hearts and often finds the truth we are trying to hide. Could it be that in the midst of some circumstances you are presently experiencing, you are trying to hold on to something while God is telling you to let go? This is, perhaps, a time for learning what is actually in your heart.

In the New Testament, James tells us that testing circumstances plus perseverance lead to a mature faith. Mature faith that results from such experiences is complete and lacks nothing for successful living (James 1:3–4). The word used for perseverance is not one that simply means "grinning and bearing the tough circumstances." Instead, it means the ability to turn difficult situations into greatness and glory. It is the ability to see through the surface of difficult situations and realize that God's hand is in the midst of those circumstances working out things for our best. William Barclay calls it "unswerving constancy."

A Challenge from History

August 22, 1741, was a sweltering day in London. A stoop-shouldered man wandered through the streets. His nightly aimless wandering through the streets of the city had become a familiar ritual. His angry mind raced back to the memories of great adulation and then looked to a future of apparently hopeless despair.

For forty years this bachelor had written operatic music that earned rave reviews throughout Europe. Honors had fallen at his feet. He was in demand everywhere.

Then the tables turned quickly and drastically. Fellow musicians became jealous and bitter. Members of the royal court turned him off like a switch. A rival gained great success, seeming to leave Handel in his dust. From every unexpected corner, the heat of trials and opposition seemed to rage with intensity.

As if these problems weren't enough, a cerebral hemorrhage paralyzed his right side. He could no longer write. Doctors gave little hope for recovery. After everything had been so good, how had it suddenly become so bad?

The composer traveled to France and began to soak in baths rumored to have miraculous powers. Doctors warned him about staying in the scalding water for such long periods, but he ignored their advice. He once stayed in the water for nine consecutive hours.

Gradually his weakened muscles began to pulse with new life. As his health improved, he began to write. Soon, to his amazement, his works were being received with rapturous applause. Life seemed to be heading for the stars. But then he found himself in the pits once more.

Queen Caroline, who had been his staunch supporter, died. England found itself on hard economic times. Wasting heat to warm a theater was viewed as ridiculous. His shows were canceled. And now he found himself wandering aimlessly through the streets once again.

Wondering where in the world God was, he wandered back home. Opening his door, he found a wealthy gentleman waiting in his living room. The man was Charles Gibbon, who had startled England by rewriting Shakespeare.

Gibbon explained that he had just finished writing text for a musical that covered the entire Old and New Testaments.

He believed the gifted musician was the man to set it to music. He gave the manuscript to the composer and challenged him to write. As he walked out the door, Gibbon turned long enough to say, "The Lord gave me those words."

The great maestro scoffed at the audacity of the young man. No one had ever challenged him, George Frederick Handel, to write something he had not thought of first. Handel's legendary violent temper was a dominating presence among his enemies. He wondered why Gibbon had brought him such a task. Why hadn't the young man brought an opera that was more his cup of tea?

He began to read, indifferently at first. Suddenly portions of the passage leaped from the page. His eyes fell on such words as, *"He was despised, rejected of men . . . he looked for someone to have pity on him, but there was no man; neither found he any to comfort him."* His eyes raced ahead to, *"He trusted in God . . .God did not leave his soul in hell . . . He will give you rest."* And finally his eyes stopped at, *"I know that my Redeemer liveth . . . rejoice . . . hallelujah."*

Handel began to write. Music flowed through his mind as though it had been penned up for years. Putting music to the script, he finished the first part in seven days. The second section was completed in nine more. Part three was completed in six days. Two days were given to fine-tuning the instrumentation.

Thus, at the age of fifty-seven, Handel completed the *Messiah* in a mere twenty-four days.

Many know that when the classical work was first performed in London and the "Hallelujah Chorus" was reached, King George II stood, apparently because he was so greatly moved. To this day people still rise to their feet as a sign of worship of God and admiration of this great work of art.

Handel, like Joseph, had to deal with life's adversities. But the strength to do so came from knowing the One who could overcome anything that life threw in his way. How about you? Do you know the God who can take you through life's fiery trials? Do you see His hand even in the flames in which you may find yourself? Very likely, the furnace is merely a brief stopping place on the road to true quality and usefulness.

Putting Yourself in the Refiner's Hands

1. Explain in your own words what it means to have a sense of destiny. Joseph had one—do you? Describe it.
2. Recall the difference between jealousy, envy, and bitterness. How do they relate to each other? Are you struggling with some or all of these in your present situation?
3. How does God use adverse circumstances in our lives? What promises has He made to us in the midst of these difficult times? What does that mean to you?

FIVE

Temptation's Fire Makes the Furnace Roar

AS WE TALKED ON THE PHONE, THE TENSION was as taut as a tug-of-war cable about to snap. My mind was reeling for an explanation. What had happened was beyond my comprehension.

I had known my friend for some time, had spoken with him on national programs, had enjoyed coffee with him as we talked and shared about God's call on our lives, and had prayed often for his marriage and family. But now I was shattered. I had just found out he had admitted to a long-standing affair which no one had suspected.

As we talked, the question that leaped from my mouth was, "How could you do it? Didn't you realize what was happening? Weren't there alarm warnings going off at least when the affair was in danger of beginning?"

His silence reminded me of a funeral home hush. After what seemed to be an interminable period, he quietly and hesitantly responded, "Yes, Bob, there were warnings. I heard the alarms of my conscience and God's Word clanging within my life . . . but I decided to disconnect the wires of the alarm."

There it was—the key truth. All of us, as we are faced with temptation, must make choices. Our choices in those moments determine not only the immediate future, but often the ramifications with which we deal for an entire lifetime.

The Road to Success Can Be a Slippery Slope to Disaster

Many people at the pinnacle of some journey, whether it's related to their career or to some other facet of life, find themselves tumbling down the slope of disaster. The road we often call "success" is unfortunately bordered by the steep terrain of temptation and the seemingly bottomless canyons of immoral and unethical decisions. Look at history—it's littered with people who made a difference but were dramatically injured, stained, and bruised by the decisions they made "in the clutch." For instance:

- Abraham followed God obediently until he lied about his wife, claiming she was just his sister, to save his own skin.
- David, at the pinnacle of his career, slept with another man's wife and then had the man murdered to cover his own wrong.
- Solomon was given arguably the greatest wisdom of any leader ever, only to break God's guidelines for living and thus see his nation shattered and divided upon his death.
- Charles Keating lost a financial empire because his greed said, "I need more."
- Jimmy Swaggart and Jim Bakker saw worldwide ministries crumble when they thought they could talk the walk without walking the talk.

- Bill Clinton lost the historical legacy he so desired only to be shackled with a legacy he would give anything to lose.

Etc., etc., ad nauseum . . .

The list is endless. It's as though, as a person rises in responsibility and opportunity, Satan turns up the heat in the furnace of temptation. Joseph was no exception.

Joseph gained his boss's attention when Potiphar bought the young man out of slavery from the Midianites and took him into his own household. Potiphar watched Joseph's consistency, competence, and character, and eventually he promoted this up-and-coming Hebrew to the position of manager of his entire estate. Since Potiphar served as one of Egypt's leading officials, Joseph suddenly found himself thrust into prominence and power.

Unfortunately, the position of success often carries a costly price tag. As Potiphar was so respected and recognized in the land, it's very possible that he reflected the typical Type A personality of aggressive leaders. While he was prominent in the land, perhaps he wasn't nearly as prominent at home. While he was seemingly always present in public, perhaps he was rarely present in private. Whatever the reality, the simple fact is, his wife became restless. Her needs were not being met at home with the husband of her youth. Emotionally, perhaps she watched her husband have "an affair" with his work. We don't know the details, but we do know that eventually Potiphar's wife set her eyes on young Joseph. The flames of temptation began to roar with intensity. Scripture describes the situation like this:

> So he [Potiphar] left in Joseph's care everything he had; with Joseph in charge, he did not concern himself with anything except the food he ate.

> Now Joseph was well-built and handsome, and after a while his master's wife took notice of Joseph and said, "Come to bed with me!"
>
> But he refused. "With me in charge," he told her, "my master does not concern himself with anything in the house; everything he owns he has entrusted to my care. No one is greater in this house than I am. My master has withheld nothing from me except you, because you are his wife. How then could I do such a wicked thing and sin against God?" And though she spoke to Joseph day after day, he refused to go to bed with her or even be with her.
>
> One day he went into the house to attend to his duties, and none of the household servants was inside. She caught him by his cloak and said, "Come to bed with me!" But he left his cloak in her hand and ran out of the house.
>
> When she saw that he had left his cloak in her hand and had run out of the house, she called her household servants. "Look," she said to them, "this Hebrew has been brought to us to make sport of us! He came in here to sleep with me, but I screamed. When he heard me scream for help, he left his cloak beside me and ran out of the house."
>
> She kept his cloak beside her until his master came home. Then she told him this story: "That Hebrew slave you brought us came to me to make sport of me. But as soon as I screamed for help, he left his cloak beside me and ran out of the house."
>
> When his master heard the story his wife told him, saying, "This is how your slave treated me," he burned with anger. Joseph's master took him and put him in prison, the place where the king's prisoners were confined. (Gen. 39:6–20)

The Furnace Roars

Perhaps there is no greater lure in all of life than that of illicit sexual liaisons. The pages of history as well as the newsbreaks of today are replete with those who have been lured into the trap of sexual infidelity. Given free reign of Potiphar's affairs, Joseph faced the temptation to "have his cake and eat it too."

It never ceases to amaze me how powerfully temptation comes knocking. Joseph had likely seen his boss's wife feeling neglected. He had daily beheld her beauty. He was young, virile, and at the height of his masculinity. And after all, Potiphar had given him access to everything else in the house. What difference would just one brief afternoon episode make anyway?

Those thoughts and more had to run through young Joseph's mind. But that's the way temptation is. It comes knocking in the most unexpected ways and in some of the most attractive packages.

Temptation doesn't usually come barging into our lives with overwhelming and sudden assaults. It's subtle. It begins with small sequential steps. Perhaps Joseph saw it begin by a seemingly innocent brush of his master's wife's hand against his own. Perhaps it was a look she gave him across the room. Or a squeeze of her hand on his shoulder unseen by those nearby. As Joseph was in and out of the house on a regular basis, perhaps his boss's wife made sure she was dressed alluringly or scantily when Joseph was around and her husband wasn't. The sequential steps of subtlety fanned the flames of temptation until they finally threatened to engulf him in the woman's blatant proposition.

Regardless of the stage of the temptation, the Bible clearly tells us, ". . . each one is tempted when, by his own evil desire, he is dragged away and enticed. Then, after desire has conceived, it gives birth to sin; and sin, when it is full-grown, gives birth to death" (James 1:14–15). The picture used here is that of an animal or a fish being baited into a trap. The bait looks so good, feels so safe, and promises to produce so much pleasure. Only when the trap snaps shut or the fish bites into the hook does the sad reality of temptation's danger strike home.

Here are some important lessons to keep in mind:

1. Temptation is inevitable. Even Christ experienced temptation. Interestingly, we find that one of His greatest temptations happened exactly when it happens for many of us—right after a pinnacle experience. The Gospels tell us that immediately after His baptism and God's clear blessing, Jesus was immediately taken into the wilderness to face a period of testing by temptation. That's how it often happens with us, as well. Devastating temptation more often comes in the wake of success than in the ditch of disappointment. Perhaps it's because when we're basking in success, we feel invincible. It's at those points of victory where we get lulled into the slumber of believing we're in control, and nothing bad or consequential could happen.

Remember, it was at the height of his reign and his popularity that David fell into immorality. It was when it looked like Gary Hart had a lock on the presidential nomination that his tryst moved from private to public. And just when Bill Clinton thought he would go down as one of America's greatest leaders, he found himself going into history books in a totally opposite way.

2. There is one, and only one, ultimate temptation. From the time of Adam and Eve to the present, while temptation seems to take many forms, there is only one root challenge—will I choose God's way or my way? Early in Genesis we find Satan tempting Eve to "be like God." The temptation to be like God tells us to take control and call our own shots. Regardless of the form of temptation, the root is always the same. Are you going to live by God's owner's manual, the Scripture, or are you going to write your own book and do your own thing?

3. No temptation comes without a price tag. I'm always amazed at how many people believe they can escape sin's consequences. Regardless of how many we see bite the dust morally, there are still people who believe they're the exception to the rule. God's Word makes it very clear. He loves us enough to warn us, saying, "Be sure that your sin will find you out" (Num. 32:23), and "A man reaps what he sows" (Gal. 6:7). Remember that if you surrender to temptation, it will take you further than you want to go, cost you more than you want to pay, and leave you emptier than you ever dreamed possible.

4. The battle with temptation is won or lost in the mind. The decisions we make, often before temptation comes, predetermine the outcome. As temptation so often enters through our visual gates, Job was wise to decide ahead of time that he would not let his eyes linger with lust on a member of the opposite sex (Job 31:1). Jesus told us the eye is the window to the soul, and therefore, we should guard carefully what enters through the panes of our windows (Matt. 6:22–23). Again, remember Satan's deception with Eve when he caused her to *look* on the fruit, because he knew the impact of visual stimulation. Where do you allow your eyes to go? Scripture clearly tells us we are to work hard at taking "captive every thought to make it obedient to Christ" (2 Cor. 10:5).

5. Giving in to temptation anesthetizes our consciences and convictions. The move to disaster is subtle rather than sudden. From one end of Scripture to the other we see that Satan places temptation in our path because he realizes, once we surrender to it, we will move closer to the second, third, fourth, and then to habitual sin. The psalmist knew the dangers of temptation's progressive nature when he warned that we should be careful of our associations. "Blessed is the man / who does not walk in the counsel of the wicked," he wrote, "or stand in the way of sinners / or sit in the seat of mockers" (Ps. 1:1).

Notice the progression demonstrated by the verbs he chose—walk, stand, and sit. General association is depicted by the word *walk*. But if we walk too often with those whose lifestyles don't reflect a relationship with God, before we know it we have stopped *walking*, and we are *standing*. We spend more and more time with those people. Pretty soon we'll be *sitting* with the wrong crowd.

It's a sedentary progression which can only be avoided if we make decisions early about how we intend to avoid this downwardly progressive spiral. If we give in, sin will inevitably cause a hardening of the heart. And once that happens, our spiritual lives will begin to deteriorate, and eventually we will lose our ability to discern what is truly right and wrong. On the other hand, every time we reject temptation, we strengthen our convictions and our spiritual muscle.

The Fight for Right

Joseph clearly understood the principles outlined in the previous section. He wasn't surprised by the heat of temptation. He knew if he yielded, he was ultimately choosing his way rather than God's. Despite the high price he paid, he truly understood that the consequences of sin would be far greater than the consequences of resisting. He won the battle with temptation in his mind. He made wise decisions before the temptation presented itself.

What do you do when you find yourself in Joseph's sandals? How do you survive the onslaught of temptation? What practical tools help you make the right decisions when the heat is on?

I've found four questions to be extremely beneficial when I'm faced with a decision between right and wrong. Most often the battleground comes not in the public arena, but in the privacy of my own heart and soul. That's where I've found these questions to be invaluable:

1. *If I participate in this activity or attitude, how will it impact me personally?* Every attitude or action affects me for the positive or negative. I am either being built up in my integrity, honesty, morality, and spirituality, or I am being torn down. There are very few neutralities. Since every action and attitude adds a brick to the structure of my life, I must be sure that the foundation and walls I am building are solid rather than faulty.

2. *If I participate in this activity or attitude, how will it affect those I care about?* If those I love most knew of my involvement, how would they feel? Would they be proud of me, or disappointed? Would it assure them of my love, or would it undermine our relationship? Would it build trust, or tear it down? Would it demonstrate my respect for them, or indicate my disregard for their feelings?

3. *If I participate in this activity or attitude, how will it affect others who watch my life?* Assuming that God's desire

for me is to make a positive difference in this world, how will my involvement affect those who are impacted by my life? Would the people I see regularly at work and other places respect me if they knew I was thinking or doing this? Would it encourage them? Would I think it was OK if I knew they were doing this thing? If it's OK for me, would I be equally happy if my spouse or my children or my parents were participating in this behavior or this attitude?

4. *If I participate in this activity or attitude, how will it affect the cause of Christ and the Christian community?* Is this attitude or activity something I am ashamed to share with my Christian community? Would I be embarrassed if my pastor knew? If the people I sit with on any given Sunday knew this was happening in my life, would it negatively or positively affect our relationship?

While we have no way of knowing what went through Joseph's mind specifically, Scripture does tell us he was keenly aware of the negative and tragic impact if he yielded to this particular temptation. He knew it would not only affect him, but also his boss, whom he evidently cared for, and ultimately it would hurt his God.

The Fight for Right in the Sexual Arena

Beyond these basic questions, let me offer some suggestions specifically for dealing with sexual temptation:

1. *Stay away from where you shouldn't be.* Our young man Joseph understood this principle. The Genesis passage we quoted earlier says that, at the height of his temptation, he refused to go to bed with his boss's wife, or *even to be with her*. In introducing the story of David's tragic affair with Bathsheba, Scripture tells us David was walking on his

palace roof when he should have been off at war. He was in the wrong place at the wrong time. As a result, he walked head-on into temptation.

So what about you? Are you ever in the wrong place at the wrong time? Do you watch movies in hotels as you travel that you shouldn't be watching? Do you read suggestive magazines or novels? Do you linger around an attractive member of the opposite sex at work, perhaps hoping you will brush against each other, even though you'll make it look like an accident? Are you searching Web sites on the Internet that contain material not conducive to moral purity?

2. Keep your eyes where they belong. Any man who has a "significant other" may have noticed the same interesting fact that I have. When you're in a public place, and a beautiful woman walks in, turning the head of every male in the establishment, have you ever watched your wife or your fiancée or your girlfriend? She won't look at the knock-out who just walked in—she will lock on your eyes. She wants to know where you will look. That's a wise reminder to keep your eyes where they belong. Remember what we noted earlier—sin often begins with the eyes.

3. Focus your thoughts on what you want to become. The writer of Proverbs summed it up well when he said, "Guard your heart, / for it is the wellspring of life" (Prov. 4:23). Remember, whatever you put into your life is inevitably what will come out. To guard your heart from adverse influences, actions, and attitudes requires a definitive act of the will. Guarding your heart requires eternal vigilance.

4. When you run headlong into sexual temptation, run for your life. There is a reason that Scripture tells us to "flee . . . youthful lusts" (2 Tim. 2:22, NKJV). Take great care to refrain from verbal intimacy with someone other than your spouse. Take great care in how you touch, hug, or contact a member of the opposite sex. Be cautious about baring your emotions to someone outside of your marriage. Understand that flirtation is intrinsically flattering and compellingly alluring, so avoid it like the plague. And when the atmosphere seems to be heating up, and the situation is becoming awkward, make a hasty exit. You can't get into trouble when you're not there!

5. Find a special friend, and give that person permission to ask you tough questions about your actions and your attitudes. I'll talk more about this later, but for now let's just say this is what real friends do. They protect you, even from yourself.

6. Remember, temptation often follows great success. This warning bears repeating. While Joseph's life clearly demonstrates this principle, let me also give a present-day example.

Super Bowl XXXIII was played in Miami. After successive losing years, suddenly Atlanta found itself playing the Broncos for the top prize in professional football. The day before the big game, Eugene Robinson was awarded the Bart Starr award for "high moral character" at a standing-room-only brunch. Everyone affirmed what an outstanding leader, Christian, and moral gentleman he was. Cameras flashed. Broadcasts went across the country. Newspapers heralded the award.

Unfortunately, that night, just twelve hours after receiving the award, Eugene was arrested not far from the team hotel. He would be charged with soliciting an undercover police officer.

Remember—no one is immune to temptation, especially when things are going well.

The Danger Zone

Sexual temptation seems to arise regularly in so many lives. But it often seems that it proliferates among leaders. These people don't have to be well-known. They need only assume a role of leadership wherever they may be serving—in the marketplace, at church, in a social club, in a volunteer organization, on a sports team, or even among a group of friends. Four major factors seem to draw sexual temptation like magnets draw iron filings:

- Power
- Personality
- Position
- Possessions

Knowing this, I would point out several dangers that anyone with even a modicum of leadership ability and responsibility will face:

1. *Don't let your success diminish your accountability.* My friend, Dr. Howard Hendricks, who teaches at Dallas Theological Seminary, did a study on a significant number of ministers who had fallen morally. When he looked for the root causes, one of the primary things he found was that all of them admitted to having no accountability in leadership. That is a disaster waiting to happen. We are not readily able to see and hear God. Therefore, we can say we are accountable to God and really be accountable to no one.

As I said earlier, it's incredibly helpful, and practically essential, to have someone in your life who can and will ask you the tough questions:

- Have you had any lustful thoughts about someone other than your spouse recently?
- Have you been tempted to do anything unethical financially?
- Are you doing anything to keep in shape physically?
- Are you having some kind of regular spiritual devotion time in your private life?
- Have you spent quality, as well as quantity, time with your family in the last month?
- Are you keeping your thought life pure and clean?
- And the real zinger—have you lied when you answered any of these questions?

Perhaps Richard Foster says it as well as it can be said when he declares, "Nothing is more dangerous than leaders accountable to no one . . . if we look at the abuses of power in Church today, very often we will see that behind them is someone who has decided that he or she has a direct pipeline to God and therefore does not need the correction of the community."[1]

2. *Avoid a lifestyle filled with hyperactivity.* Increasingly in modern life, we have effectively substituted busyness for godliness. We are convinced that activity must equate spirituality. The drier we've become internally, the busier we've become externally.

Bill Hybels is respected by the Christian community for his gifts of leadership and his motivation to build one of America's largest churches. But Bill readily admits that in the 1980s he almost lost his ministry and his marriage. He describes the days in which hyperactivity kept him going at breakneck speed. I heard him say one time, "There came a point in my life where the work of the church around me began to kill the work of God within me."

When we refuse to stop for times of refueling—spiritually, physically, and emotionally—inevitably the gauges of our lives fall into the danger zone. What was once the fuel of reality becomes only the fumes of memory. What was once fresh becomes stale. When we realize something is wrong, our first answer is "But I don't have time to get things in order . . ."

3. Don't succumb to the lifestyle of celebrity. You don't have to be famous to find yourself in a celebrity posture. Perhaps you single-handedly set a new sales record for your company. Perhaps you won a significant case for your law firm. Perhaps your recent weight loss or your new clothes or hairstyle created an instant sensation. Perhaps an unexpected inheritance thrust you into financial opportunity.

Regardless of how it's packaged, when an individual suddenly seems blessed with abundance in popularity, finances, emotional strength, good looks, etc., that person has entered a unique danger zone for temptation.

We shouldn't be surprised at this—after all, God warned us about it in His Word. In Deuteronomy 8, He told Israel that, after they had gone into the Promised Land and found things going well, it was essential that they exercise great caution. Why? Because He knew human nature. When things start going our way, and suddenly we find ourselves in the spotlight of success, we tend to forget our Source—God. Suddenly we begin to think we earned it—we accomplished it—we provided it. Or, perhaps most deadly of all—we come to believe we deserve it. That's when we forget God, drop our guard, and invite catastrophe.

Don't Disconnect the Alarm!

Joseph had a terrific spiritual alarm system. Scripture doesn't specifically tell us how he got it. Certainly, it didn't come from imitating his parents or his older siblings. He didn't have God's written Word to serve as a guide. We can only guess that he gained a certain clarity in his spiritual eyes and ears while God was molding him in the crucible of adversity.

But the bottom line is that, even up until the last minute when Potiphar's wife harassed and tried to seduce him, he could have turned off the alarm. It's a relatively easy thing to do. Yet, as in a steel forging plant, the alarm sounds when the fire gets too hot. Ignore it, and you will be burned at best—destroyed at worst.

Joseph refused to succumb to temptation. He let the alarm ring loudly and clearly, and he responded by fleeing from the lure of sin. When God loves you enough to give you an internal warning about the danger of temptation, listen to the alarm!

Joseph's actions in the face of such intense sexual temptation stand as a wonderful example of what the apostle Paul meant when he wrote, "God is faithful; he will not let you be tempted beyond what you can bear. But when you are tempted, he will also provide a way out so that you can stand up under it" (1 Cor. 10:13). So, the next time He sets the alarm to ringing, and He provides a way out as He's promised, remember—it's up to you to take the exit.

Putting Yourself in the Refiner's Hands

1. List some places you know you shouldn't go, given your specific weaknesses. What measures will you take to make sure you stay away from those places?

2. Since we've agreed that temptation often comes through visual contact, what practical, specific steps do you intend to take to guard your eyes?

3. List one or two friends you can trust with the intimate details of your life. Ask them to hold you accountable for your behavior—Be willing to have them ask you life's "tough questions."

4. Relaxed Schedule Overwhelming Schedule

   1 2 3 4 5 6 7 8 9 10

   Rate yourself from 1–10 by circling the number that best describes your current level of busyness. Evaluate your lifestyle. Are you too busy? What is that doing to your God-given "alarm system?"

5. What practical and specific things are you doing to keep your personal alarm system in good working order?

SIX

Burned by Unjust Accusations

SOON AFTER MY PARENTS ENROLLED ME IN kindergarten, I became a regular tenant of the "unhappy room" (my creative teacher's version of "the corner"). I should have just signed a lease and paid rent, because as I recall, a healthy portion of each and every day was relegated to this character-building routine. Apparently my teacher didn't approve of such varied and sundry activities as putting frogs in her desk and pulling fire alarms.

My reputation preceded my appearance in first grade. Miss Nendle awaited my arrival with a jaundiced eye. And who was I to disappoint her? Each day my mother met me at the door of our home with the teacher's report of my latest dastardly deeds. Unfortunately, all the reports could have been labeled "true and confirmed."

And then it happened. Eventually I was accused of something I really didn't do—honest!

Marilyn, a girl in our class, was big for her age. In fact, according to my childhood memories, I would say she could have started on most high school football teams. At recess, some of the fellows decided to ever-so-gently let Marilyn know what they thought of her. In the loving sensitivity of typical first graders, they called out, "Hey, Baby Huey! You can get a job as the Goodyear blimp when you grow up."

Well, that statement produced a mental picture that simply couldn't be contained. I collapsed with laughter. I could actually see her suspended in the clouds. And then I felt the ground shake. Marilyn was thundering toward our little group, and my wonderful, faithful, courageous, self-sacrificing friends pointed at me and quickly volunteered, "He said it."

Of course, it wasn't true, but Marilyn still cleaned my clock. As I lay prostrate under the barrage of Marilyn's fists and fingernails, I remember swearing that I would get even with my alleged friends if it was the last thing I ever did. Unjust accusation had caught me by surprise.

Joseph could have identified with me to some degree. Or, more realistically, I could identify with him. But, while I had justly earned a reputation that seemed to support my friends' fingerpointing, Joseph had not. Scripture indicates he was clean and pure. He simply accepted and even tried to make the best of every situation. And then, just when he seemed destined for higher things, the bottom fell out once again for young Joseph. He was unjustly accused of a terrible crime.

Joseph's Story

The previous chapter described Joseph's temptation to engage in a sexual liaison with his boss's wife. It outlined his refusal to comply with her proposition, and it touched briefly on the results of that encounter.

Things fell apart for Joseph that day. He tore himself away from Potiphar's wife, leaving his jacket hanging in her hands. She began screaming, and, using his jacket as evidence, she accused him of attempted rape. Joseph ended up in jail.

The good life had seemingly turned its back on Joseph once again. How was it possible that he could live so right, and things could still go so wrong? Was life ever fair?

Well, the answer is no—it wasn't fair. And it still isn't. But Scripture doesn't tell us life will always be fair. Some of God's greatest people have suffered tremendously from unjust situations. The children of Israel unjustly accused Moses of improper leadership. Saul unjustly attacked David, whom he saw as a threat. And what greater illustration of unjust accusation is there than those remarks hurled against our Lord Himself?

You probably haven't been accused of attempting to seduce your boss's spouse, or your boss. But chances are you've had some sort of encounter with false accusation. It's easy enough to identify with Joseph's predicament. For you, the circumstances may have been different, but the results were still hurtful and maybe even disastrous.

Perhaps production parts at the job were damaged and someone fingered you to take the fall. Perhaps a vital report was lost and, since you were the one who typed it, you were the culprit. Maybe a project was mentioned in conversation by your boss (but never assigned). Now he wants to know why you have not completed it. Or maybe you were given a specific project. The problem was, though given the responsibility for the job, you weren't given the needed authority. Now they want your head on a platter. Closer to home, maybe your seven-year-old assaults you with the accusation,

"You're just not fair. All my friends get to do it. You're the meanest parent I've ever seen."

Why Do People Make Accusations That Aren't True?

Regardless of the particular situation, why does false accusation occur? Obviously, we need to understand root causes in order to deal with effects. Several of these causes are evident in Joseph's situation.

1. *Unjust accusation can come from an attempt to cover wrongdoing.* This may have been the reason Potiphar's wife accused Joseph of attempted rape. Her advances had been rejected. Her fantasy affair had not materialized. Just in case her flirtatious conduct backfired, she wanted to be covered. The motto "the best defense is a good offense" was fleshed out in her treacherous dealings. Unfortunately, it was Joseph's flesh at stake.

No one ever wants to be found in the wrong. We don't have to wait long in life to witness this reality. If our children's rooms look like a tornado just moved through, it is always their "friend" who did the damage. If someone's feelings get trampled as children are playing, it requires a slow motion replay to follow the hands as accusing fingers are pointed at each other. If an expensive lamp is knocked over and broken, the culprit is always the younger brother or sister, or the dog. Self-preservation can be an incredibly strong motive.

2. *Sometimes false accusations rise from a desire to punish others for refusing to go along.* Joseph avoided the advances of Potiphar's wife, perhaps even making her feel unattractive. Her motivation for accusing him may have been a desire to punish him for his refusal.

Pressure to "go along to get along" can be overpowering. Kids face it every day at school. Executives face it daily in the marketplace. Women fighting for advancement on the job are pounded with it. When someone finds the strength to stand up to this type of pressure, it can infuriate those applying it. A "no" can be taken as a personal affront by those attempting to put us in a compromising position.

In actuality, those doing the tempting often wish (perhaps subconsciously) they had the strength to refuse as well. Not having that kind of fortitude, though, their perception of reality is blurred. All of us detest rejection—perceived or real. People respond by setting out to get even. Joseph was caught in this very trap.

3. Some people give in to a temptation to make themselves look better than others. Being innately manipulative creatures, we humans are tempted to do whatever it takes to allow us to come out on top. The temptation is to look out for "number one." Some feel power can be achieved through intimidation. Still others think they can raise their own status by putting someone else down.

This doesn't always require raw accusatory statements. Sometimes we can simply allow another individual to be falsely blamed. We know the facts, yet we remain silent. Open-ended statements can also crucify the character of another. How easy it is to say that a fellow executive left for lunch with his secretary, not bothering to include that four others went with them.

I heard a story about a first officer of a navy vessel who had a major disagreement with his captain concerning a problem aboard ship. The captain eventually had to pull rank and give a direct command. Disliking the command, the first officer purposely delayed its execution. In response to the disobedience, the captain recorded in the ship's log, "Today the first officer exhibited insubordination."

The first officer became vindictive. Wanting to make the captain look bad while elevating himself, he wrote in the ship's log: "Today the captain was sober." What he failed to say was that the captain was sober every day. The pressure to make oneself look good at someone else's expense can be overpowering.

4. Some people merely have the determination to manipulate. False accusation, or the threat of such accusation, can carry great manipulative power—almost like blackmail. An unscrupulous person may threaten to revive old secrets from the past or to exploit weaknesses. Strong, domineering personalities may find great pleasure in making puppets of those with weaker constitutions. This is the ultimate in wickedness. Such wickedness characterized Potiphar's wife, whose desire was to manipulate Joseph.

Things are not always as they appear. That's why it is important to gain understanding, at least in part, as to where accusations originate. Such understanding enables us to better deal with them. Joseph is a perfect model, because he had developed the type of character capable of handling such flagrant attacks.

What Joseph Did

In the quietness of his early life, Joseph had godly qualities ingrained into his character. Many of these character traits probably were learned at Rachel's knee. Others came from observing the radical change in his father after a life-altering night of wrestling with God. These qualities had already aided him when he was in the treacherous hands of his brothers. He called on them again when he was framed.

Though written Scripture was still in the future, its principles were evidenced in Joseph's life. He had, undoubtedly, heard stories of men like Enoch and Noah and Abraham. He knew how they had walked with God. And, having witnessed his father's deceitfulness and self-centeredness during his early life, Joseph must have marveled at the changed man who returned from Jabbok. A God who could cause that kind of change in a man—that was the God upon whom Joseph wanted to build his life.

Even when Joseph no longer had any of his family or friends around him, he still had God. This is the one relationship that neither geography nor circumstance can ever take from us. It was God's presence that saw Joseph through the dark night of his soul when he was falsely accused by Potiphar's wife.

Joseph's position in Potiphar's service was increased until he rose to the position of chief steward of the household. Potiphar knew that in Joseph he had a trustworthy servant to oversee and care for his estate. Because of his insight, God blessed Potiphar's house (Gen. 39:5), even though he was an Egyptian and did not know Joseph's Lord.

But all was not well in Potiphar's home. Potiphar's wife noticed something more than Joseph's administrative skills. She noticed Joseph for a different reason; she saw him as a handsome male servant living and working in her home who might be available to satisfy her unfulfilled sexual desires.

Potiphar's wife repeatedly attempted to lure Joseph into having an adulterous liaison. Lust had gone to her head and the clothes of modesty were thrown aside. Her sense of decency, her reputation, and her moral conscience were all disregarded, as they usually are when one is overcome by and possessed with the desires of the flesh. But Joseph resisted her charms, invitations, and shameless solicitations.

Day after day, Joseph was, by the grace of God, able to resist and overcome this terrible temptation. How easy it would have been to obey her, considering the circumstances. He was living in a luxurious estate, he was single, he was healthy, and he was her slave—it was his duty to obey and in his best interest to oblige in whatever she requested. Her feminine beauty, charm, and soft invitations to possess her completely were constantly confronting him. Confined to work and living under the same roof with this woman and her open invitation to have a sexual affair must have been virtually unbearable for him.

Furthermore, in light of the knowledge of the unsatisfactory nature of her marital relations with Potiphar, he might have justified going to bed with her as an "act of service" to meet the needs of the mistress of the household. Can you conceive of a greater array of rationalizations than were at hand in this situation before Joseph? He knew his rejection of her invitations was offending her; but regardless of her reaction, Joseph continued to refuse and avoid her. She, however, was determined and would not give up.

She brought the situation to a climax when she tried, one last time, to seduce Joseph.

No one besides Joseph was in the home that day. There may have been other servants in the house, but because of their position as slaves they would not have paid any attention to what she was doing. She felt especially daring and shameless that day when she sought him out in the house. With a determined face and even more focused demeanor, she grasped Joseph by his garment and screamed, "Lie with me!" (Gen. 39:12, NKJV)

Joseph realized the danger of the situation when she must have appeared to him to be pulling off his clothes. He fled, she clung, and Joseph ran out of the house at least partially disrobed.

Her passion instantly turned to rage. Knowing now that her passion for Joseph would never be fulfilled, her only thought was how to humiliate him as fully as possible.

She was overcome with anger. She sat there a moment thinking, and fuming—he had refused her for the very last time. She calmed down and collected her thoughts. He must pay for this—but how? Suddenly it dawned on her: her knuckles were white as she loosened her grip—his garment was still in her hand!

If Potiphar walked in now, it would be terribly incriminating for her. Unless, of course, she could turn the tables in her own favor and make her possession of this robe incriminating evidence against Joseph. Yes, that was it! She determined to frame him—she breathed deeply and directed all her rage outwardly as she screamed, "Rape!" Instantly the other servants came running to attend to her.

When Potiphar came home she was ready to weave a testimony that would, by law, bring Joseph the death penalty. In effect, she placed the blame on her husband: she told Potiphar how this man, this "Hebrew" that he had allowed into his home and promoted to chief steward, had attempted to rape the very mistress of the household. How fortunate he should be, however, that she had barely saved herself from being overpowered by this "rapist" by screaming so loudly that she frightened him away. He ran out so quickly that he left some of his clothes. How relieved he should be, as her husband, that his precious and "innocent" wife had escaped this horrible slave's violent hand.

Upon hearing her story, Potiphar was rightly incensed. Joseph was evidently found and brought back to Potiphar. But isn't it curious that there is no indication Joseph ever attempted to defend himself against the false charges. Why? There are several possible reasons he didn't defend himself. First of all, there was the social/political situation—Egyptians would not have allowed the word of a mere slave to be taken over and against the word of Potiphar's wife. Or Joseph may have actually been such a loyal servant (based on his integrity that was grounded in his faith in his God) that he felt compelled to protect the reputation of his mistress—a purely objective decision given her depravity and wickedness toward him.

What happens next is also interesting. Instead of being condemned and executed, Joseph was thrown into a prison. Actually, it was not a prison for criminals. This was a prison that held political prisoners; ironically, none other than Potiphar himself was the government official who oversaw this prison. Thus God saved Joseph from death once again.

Even when he was facing such terrible false accusations in Egypt in the home of Potiphar, we see God leading Joseph through more of the fires which refined, purified, and strengthened his character.

That same God etched the maxims of godly living into Joseph's heart. He was, therefore, equipped to face his new test. Even before it was written, Joseph's life evidenced the guidelines established in Psalm 1:1–3, 6. We glanced at this passage in the previous chapter, but its richness certainly warrants another look: "Blessed is the man / who does not walk in the counsel of the wicked / or stand in the way of sinners / or sit in the seat of mockers. / But his delight is in the law of the LORD, / and on his law he meditates day and night. / He is like a tree planted by streams of water, / which yields its fruit in season / and whose leaf does not wither. / Whatever he does prospers . . . / For the LORD watches over the way of the righteous."

Notice the guidelines described in that passage.

1. God's man or woman carefully chooses companions. A person who seeks God's blessing must navigate wisely through the crowd and carefully select his or her friends and associates. Certainly, God understands that we cannot fully separate ourselves from people who may influence us negatively. In fact, He intends that we will continue to rub shoulders with non-Christians for the purpose of introducing them to Him. In other words, His intention is that the world would become more like us—not that we would become more like the world.

However, we must come to understand that a friend is very different from an acquaintance. It's always wise to surround yourself with a peer group that will hold you accountable for your behavior and will encourage rather than tear down your good moral character.

2. The people God calls "wicked" may surprise you. You see, in the original Hebrew language, the word used for *wicked* in this passage actually means a person who is determined to live by his or her own standards. This person may call on God in an emergency situation, but for the most part, God's direction or intention might as well not exist. This person's theme song would be "I Did It My Way."

By this definition the wicked are all around us, for it basically fits every secular man or woman, and many who claim to be Christian as well. Let me describe this individual. He or she is confident—possibly involved in physical fitness—a mover and a shaker. His or her daily devotional material may be the *Wall Street Journal.* Or this person may be a quiet, behind-the-scenes manipulator. He or she may be your boss, your colleague, your neighbor next door, or the person who checks you out at the grocery counter. This person takes little or no time to deeply consider the implications of expressing faith in a living God. This passage basically tells us to stay away from developing any close ties with that type of person.

3. Choosing the wrong companions has the tendency to push an individual into a downward progression. The psalmist creatively outlines this progression as he describes the "body language" of the person who chooses to "hang out with the wrong crowd." In the previous chapter, we talked about the progression from *walking* to *standing* to *sitting.* It's a continual tendency to linger longer with those who would try to blur our personal lines of right and wrong.

When we finally reach the point where we are *sitting,* we find ourselves in the company of those who claim religion is for "Holy Joes" and for weaklings who need emotional crutches. They are "mockers." Their rejection of God's principles may be subtle. They may simply cast doubt on the Bible as truly being God's Word. They may claim that church is a great place to be on Sunday, but it has no relevance for the rest of the week. Even Sunday can be excused if the opportunity comes to play golf, play tennis, or leave town. Christianity becomes, at best, a religion of convenience.

An individual who submits to this kind of activity, who drifts from walking to standing to sitting, is in great danger.

This person eventually will step off the right path, and he or she will engage in conduct that a healthy, biblically based conscience would condemn. Eventually the conscience will be so drugged and scarred that this person can sit at the banquet of sinful pleasure with no feelings of guilt.

Joseph instinctively knew he could not allow himself to walk, stand, or sit in the presence of those whose lives were not committed to his God. So he ran quickly from Potiphar's wife.

His prayer could have echoed that of the psalmist who later wrote, "Teach me your way, O LORD; / lead me in a straight path / because of my oppressors" (Ps. 27:11). Joseph had learned a lesson that we must learn as well. He knew that the man who obeys God's principles will be able to cope with life's injustices. Joseph's life was guided by obedience. He didn't walk with the wicked—he chose to walk with God and run from the wicked. And his fellowship with His Lord was close, perhaps even closer in the midst of adversity. God was very much a part of his daily life.

4. *The person who carefully chooses his companions and who obeys the principles established in God's Word will be successful.* The psalmist promises, "He is like a tree planted by streams of water, / which yields its fruit in season / and whose leaf does not wither. / Whatever he does prospers . . . / For the Lord watches over the way of the righteous" (Ps. 1:3, 6).

I once drove through a marshy area of South Carolina after extremely high winds had ravaged the area. A beautiful, stately tree had toppled beside the road. Observing its size, I judged it had stood as a tall sentinel for some time. But the wind had come with a one-two combination and put the tree down for the count.

Looking closer, I discovered an interesting phenomenon. Though the tree had experienced a good and long life, the root system was amazingly shallow. It had not drilled its way to solid ground. It had remained in the soft, moist, unstable layers of the marsh. I couldn't help thinking how many lives I had seen just like that. They didn't look bad on top, but they had no solid root system.

God's Word says the person who carefully selects his companions and obeys Scriptural principles will have a stable and successful life. He will resemble a strong, firmly rooted tree that can withstand the fury of hurricanes, and perhaps even offer shelter to others who are less firmly situated. In a country where idolatry was the main theology, Joseph carefully guarded his relationship with God. He refused to walk in the counsel of Potiphar's wife. Nor did he stand and linger in the influence of her temptations. He fled from her siren song. His steps were ordered by God's principles. His anchor was strong in the face of falsehood.

What Joseph Didn't Do

We've already looked at what Joseph did in response to Potiphar's wife. Now we should look at the things he didn't do. Those things are important, too, for they provide additional insight into how he coped with his dilemma.

1. Joseph did not doubt God's activity. Though circumstances appeared bleak, he looked through them to find God's hand at work. The story of his life was being written by the invisible hand that is always in control of the plot line. God's silence at certain points does not reflect His level of activity.

The psalmist could have had Joseph in mind when he wrote, "Do not fret because of evil men / or be envious of those who do wrong; / for like the grass they will soon wither, / like green plants they will soon die away. / Commit your way to the LORD; / trust in him and he will do this: / He will make your righteousness shine like the dawn, / the justice of your cause like the noonday sun" (Ps. 37:1–2, 5–6).

As far as we know, Joseph did not doubt that God's hand was at work backstage. His delight was in being God's man. His way was committed. There was no need to be anxious.

2. Joseph did not react with anger. I have to confess, I would have been furious. I would have told Potiphar a thing or two. But Joseph, like Christ, kept quiet when accused. What would have been gained by attempting to destroy his superior's wife? Would he have been better off? He would, possibly, have been worse off.

Scripture teaches this principle: "A fool gives full vent to his anger, / but a wise man keeps himself under control" (Prov. 29:11).[1] Given that kind of biblical injunction, we need to follow Joseph's example. We need to weigh our actions before we explode; think before we speak; be sure our mind is in gear before our mouth is in motion. We should always ask, "Will what I say make matters worse? Could it destroy someone else?"

Instead of reacting negatively, Joseph responded with kindness. He did not implicate his boss's wife. He also refused to let the incident destroy his trust in God. Further, he continued to serve with excellence. I dare to believe that he may have even prayed for his accuser. Christ would set forth this precept later when He declared, "You have heard that it was said, 'Love your neighbor and hate your enemy.' But I tell you: Love your enemies and pray for those who persecute you, that you may be sons of your Father in heaven . . ." (Matt. 5:43–45).

That's difficult to do, of course. It's so much easier to resent, be bitter, and react. Joseph set a tremendous example for us, but it's terribly difficult to follow it.

3. Joseph did not step in and take charge. Joseph trusted God to settle the score. And God, indeed, did. Eventually God placed Joseph in a far greater position than he had with Potiphar. In the end, the final act should always be God's. He promises, "A false witness will not go unpunished, / and he who pours out lies will perish" (Prov. 19:9). He also tells us through Paul, "Do not take revenge, my friends, but leave room for God's wrath, for it is written: 'It is mine to avenge; I will repay,' says the Lord" (Rom. 12:19).

Joseph's life is a challenging example, but it doesn't do much good to read it, assume we can't measure up, and then return to our old habits. Joseph proved that an ordinary man, even if he is caught in extraordinary circumstances, can live out the principles God says will make us successful in His eyes and avoid being burned by unjust accusations.

So take a minute and consider this—are the principles that governed Joseph's life also governing yours? Are you prepared to handle false accusation as well as Joseph did? Or are your roots so shallow that the onslaught of false attack may uproot you? God is able to redeem every difficulty that we endure because of false accusation. He is able to work out everything according to His purpose. And His purpose is always for our eternal good. But it's really much easier for Him to do that if we have the fortitude to stay out of His way.

Putting Yourself in the Refiner's Hands

1. Does faithfully following God guarantee a trouble-free life? Why or why not?

2. What does Psalm 1 teach about choosing friendships? Can you apply this successfully to your present friendships?
3. Have you ever been falsely accused? Describe the situation. How did you react toward the one making the false accusation? How did you respond to those believing the false accusation?

SEVEN

When the Pressure Builds

HE HAD COMMITTED MURDER. AT LEAST THAT'S what the person who phoned me said.

Bobby was the father of two children who attended our church. The pressures of failure, disappointment, and bad decisions had escalated to the "danger zone" . . . and finally exploded in violent tragedy.

The night before, in a drunken stupor, he had allegedly killed his estranged wife and wounded another man. Then he went to his wife's home and took their two children. By crossing state lines to avoid arrest, he had committed a federal offense—kidnapping. The authorities captured Bobby and took him to the county jail. The caller asked if I would visit him, to see if I could be of any help.

A multitude of reasons why I couldn't go raced through my mind. They were "important" reasons too. A football game was coming on TV. I needed to trim my fingernails. I had to take out the trash.

I came up with a hundred excuses, but none really held water. The truth was, I just didn't want to go.

You see, I could picture this guy. I knew he had to be at least 6-feet, 8-inches tall and about 240 pounds. I was sure he would have matted hair and wild, savage, bloodshot eyes. I could close my eyes and see the sinister curl to his lips.

Finally my spiritual side won out over my carnal, and I went to the jail. I was escorted to a visitation cell. The slamming door gave a chilling note of finality to the whole experience. Shaking (but undoubtedly looking together on the outside), I waited. Finally, after an eternity of about four minutes, a guard ushered Bobby into the room.

He stood there, medium height and weight. He was clean and neat. His smile sparkled. Overall he was a very handsome young man—not at all what I had anticipated.

As we began to talk, Bobby's hurt and disappointment rolled out. A broken marriage. Infidelity. Slavery to alcohol. And that was the nice, tame part of it. As the conversation progressed, I shared the difference Christ could make for him. He asked intelligent questions and made pertinent points. After two hours, he asked Christ into his life.

Bobby was convicted and sent to prison. Years later, when I traveled through Houston, I rented a car and drove to the prison where he was incarcerated. I asked Bobby his feelings about being behind bars. His answer is indelibly imprinted in my mind.

"Pastor," he said, "I am freer inside these bars than many people are outside of them. Though I'm incarcerated physically, many of them are in prisons far more terrible than mine. One day I'll be released. Some of the people on the outside may never escape from their own prisons."

Prisons Come in All Shapes and Sizes

Joseph would have understood Bobby's statement even better than I did. Unlike Bobby, of course, Joseph was imprisoned on trumped-up charges. Yet he didn't allow the injustice to destroy him. He experienced freedom despite his imprisonment, discovering one can be in limited circumstances and yet remain liberated.

As I watch people around me moving freely, I can't help but wonder how many of them are peering out from behind invisible bars. How many pressures have been building inside, like an overheated blast furnace? Many are silently immobilized by the stress of life's journey. Rather than a joyful experience, life has taken on the ugly strain of bondage. Others lash out at everything and everyone, as the pressure gauges of their internal furnaces sound a shrill warning.

Pressure and prison experiences come in different forms for different people. At eighteen years of age, my daughter Christy was a nationally ranked soccer player. As a sophomore she was a key catalyst in helping her high school team finish second in the state of Florida.

As we moved to Virginia just prior to her junior year, she found herself stepping into a totally undeveloped soccer program. She may have been tempted to throw in the towel and give up. Instead she jumped in and helped her new team win the county and district championships. In addition, she was chosen to the first team All-Tidewater, first team All-State, and the Olympic development team.

That's when the bottom fell out.

Suddenly she began to pass out at the soccer field. Doctors determined she had severe and advanced mononucleosis. That seemed to escalate into seizure disorders and a condition called neuroally mediated hypotension, where the body's extremities do not get as much blood as they need. Add to that a developing case of asthma and severe dairy allergies, and she faced the loss of her soccer career. She would be out of soccer for three years due to health reasons. Her mother, Cheryl, and I would at times literally have to carry her to the bathroom, as she could not walk on her own.

I watched this vibrant and happy athlete go from racing through opposition down the field and scoring goals to a young lady just attempting to get enough energy to make it to the dinner table. Some six years later, I had the opportunity to take her to dinner—just the two of us. We sat back and reviewed everything that had happened to her. All the disappointments. All the heartaches. All the physical difficulties . . . not to mention the emotional ones. I couldn't help but have some tears run down my cheeks as I recounted with her the vast battles she had faced.

But when it was all said and done, and I asked what came to her mind most as she looked back over the journey, she replied, "If I had it to do all over again, and had to choose between going to a major college and having a spectacular career and possibly even going to the Olympics or winning a World Cup, or going through all the valleys and disappointments and yet have what God has taught me and accomplished within me, I would take the valleys." That's when I knew my daughter had moved from being a young girl to being a mature woman of faith. There's not much more a dad could ever desire.

Pressure Points

Christy's prison experience began with a physical problem. But certainly every individual who's been in any kind of "prison" has a unique story. Let's look at a few examples:

1. Circumstances. Many find that circumstances seem to hinder their fulfillment. Nothing ever goes right. They succumb to the "grass-is-greener" syndrome.

While living in Florida, I directed the national training ministry for a rapidly growing Christian organization. My responsibilities took me all over the country. When being introduced prior to speaking, someone would inevitably mention that I lived in Fort Lauderdale. After I spoke once in Seattle, Washington, a man came up and said, "So you're from Fort Lauderdale. I wish I could live down there. Things just aren't going well for me here. Life would be easier there . . . and problems would have to be fewer. Circumstances here just aren't right."

Back home a few days later, I was doing some yard work. While practicing the fine art of horticulture, I conversed with a neighbor who was also working in his yard. With a friendly wave I greeted him and asked him how things were going. He shrugged and asked where I had been. When I told him, his response was almost verbatim to that of the man in Seattle.

"So you've been to Seattle, huh? I'd love to be in Seattle. Things just aren't going very well for me here, but I bet if I was in a place like that, things would be going great."

You may laugh, just like I did, but this story characterizes many of us very well. We always think a change in circumstances will solve the challenges we face. Paul's outlook was entirely different when he wrote, "Give thanks in all circumstances, for this is God's will for you in Christ Jesus" (1 Thess. 5:18). When we allow circumstances to master us, rather than understanding that the Master is in charge of our circumstances, we become imprisoned.

2. *Others' expectations.* Many years ago Harvard psychologist Robert Rosenthal performed an intriguing experiment regarding children's performance and teachers' expectations. He tested a group of children and assigned them at random to teachers who thought they were exceptional students, since they were labeled "spurters." At the end of the school year, he tested the children again, with astounding results. They gained as many as fifteen to twenty-seven IQ points. Because the teachers expected more from these "spurters," the children came to expect more of themselves.

My wife, who is wonderful with children, saw this principle manifested early in her teaching career. Cheryl was assigned to a school in a low socioeconomic area of Dallas. One little girl, Julie, had already been labeled a "real troublemaker." Based on assessment by other teachers, Cheryl began to expect the worst from Julie. To say that things didn't go well would be a gross understatement.

Cheryl began to look for creative ways to influence Julie's behavior. The school administration encouraged teachers to establish positive communication with the families. One day Julie went out of her way to help my wife accomplish a task—a rare event for this child. Cheryl wrote a gracious note to the mother, praising Julie for what she had done in class. The change that followed was incredible. Julie became a sweet, supportive, and cooperative student.

Finally, unable to stand the suspense any longer, Cheryl asked Julie to stop by her desk following class. She asked what had caused the change. The child grinned. "Your note to my mama," she said. "You told my mother I was good, so now I have to be."

Goethe, the famous German writer, said, "Treat people as if they are what they ought to be and you will help them become what they are capable of becoming." Many people are imprisoned because of the views or expectations of other people. What's worse, perhaps many of us put others "in prison" by the expectations we force upon them.

3. *Lack of confidence.* When I worked in Detroit, in the midst of the automobile industry, I often heard this quote attributed to Henry Ford: "Think you can, think you can't; either way you are right."

Too many of us sport a defeated attitude. We feel we cannot make a meaningful contribution or accomplish a meaningful task. We are paralyzed by the fear of taking risks. James Bryant Conant, the distinguished president of Harvard, challenged us all when he said, "Behold the turtle—he makes progress only when he sticks his neck out." Yet, we tuck in our necks and seek only to be comfortable.

Leslie Dobbins understands both the difficulty and the necessity of sticking your neck out. Les shared some difficult times in his childhood. His family had just moved, and he had extreme difficulty making friends. "Everyone had their group, and I didn't fit," he explained. While sitting in his sixth grade class, Les bent over to pick up a pencil from the floor. A young boy whom he thought was a friend leaned over and said, "You think I like you? Nobody likes you. Nobody's your friend."

Wounded. Devastated. Lonely. Les began to feel that he was drowning in a sense of personal failure. Kids can be so cruel, their wounds so deep, and the hurt so excruciating.

Fourteen years passed, each one filled with the heated pressure of loneliness and rejection. Amazingly, those two qualities can make one feel alone even in a crowd. It was toward the end of that fourteen years that life took a drastic turn for Les—he met Miss Bertha Smith, a retired missionary from China.

Anyone who was ever around Miss Bertha remembers that it was like stepping into the Lord's presence. She radiated God's love and His power. Sensing the hurt and rejection in Les, with her arm around his shoulder and her eyes looking into his, she said, "God loves you just the way you are and has accepted you in His beloved Son. You can trust Him with your present. You can trust Him with your future. And you can trust Him with other people. He wants to help you do His ministry."

Les says that's the day that turned the whole course of his life. Since then, he's served for many years in ministry. He still admits, however, "I struggled for years with the feelings of inadequacy. I learned that most of my fears were based on the feelings of failure as opposed to the fact of God's Word. When I got my beliefs in order with the Word of God, I realized that my relationship with Him is what brings true adequacy. Having learned that, I understood what it meant when the Scripture says, 'Then you will know the truth, and the truth will set you free'" (John 8:32).

In having walked through that fire, Les now serves as a Southern Baptist missionary with the North American Mission Board. He constantly finds opportunities to minister to people struggling with their own sense of inadequacy, and from the pressures and heat of the cruelty of the words of others. Isn't it amazing how God never wastes an experience in our lives . . . even the ones that bring pain?

4. Guilt. Many of us walk around with a heavy burden labeled "guilt." Old actions and reactions play a haunting refrain in the conscience. Though others may have forgiven us, often we haven't forgiven ourselves. I believe the worst type of guilt is false guilt, often generated by cultural Christianity. Too often people struggle under a Christianity that has been reduced to a list of do's and don'ts (with emphasis on the don'ts). The list becomes too heavy to bear, especially since many of the rules aren't even biblically based.

5. *Loneliness.* While today's average American meets as many people in one year as the average person did in a lifetime seventy-five years ago, too often he or she is far lonelier. This has happened for a variety of reasons, not the least of which is our increasing mobility. We move to new localities so regularly that we rarely have a real opportunity to belong to any specific community. Many of us have lost the support network of living near immediate family members, let alone extended family members. Some have substituted a network of Internet friends, but the bottom line is that there is no substitute for face-to-face communication and belonging. Without it we will feel lonely—even in a crowd. And it's devastating. Some psychiatrists who deal with depressed people have found that a human being is the only species that cannot survive alone; a human needs other human beings—otherwise he would die.

6. *Pessimism.* Many of us are walking through life imprisoned with an outlook that expects the worse. We are like the man who wore an emergency bracelet inscribed with these words: "In case of accident . . . I'm not surprised!" When we move through life expecting the worst, we usually find it.

Regardless of the Prison's Form, Freedom Is Available

Regardless of the form each "prison experience" takes, Joseph's story provides insights for coping. Look at his circumstances and remember that he was as human as we are.

To think he went into incarceration with a silly, pious grin on his face is ridiculous. Put yourself in his place. How do you think he really felt? I've used my imagination, and here's what I think.

1. *He felt abandoned.* He had given himself fully to his job. As estate administrator for Potiphar, he had not only proved to be an excellent executive, but he also established himself as an outstandingly ethical person. Still, Joseph found himself totally abandoned in a dark, dank cell. When we find ourselves in a prison experience, we usually feel abandoned as well—like no one really cares.

2. *He felt a sense of doom.* The charges were serious. Egyptian law required the death penalty for such a crime. The fact that he found himself in prison was, perhaps, an indication that Potiphar didn't totally believe his wife's story. Regardless, Joseph had to believe he might die in this prison. I'm sure we understand the sense of hopelessness that seemed to suffocate him. When life closes in, we feel as though there is no escape. Circumstances become a trap rather than a means to fulfillment.

3. *He probably felt forgotten.* Despite his loyal service and outstanding track record, no one seemed to remember him. Visitors were probably rare, if they came at all. Perhaps he even felt that God had forgotten him. He could have identified with David of later years, who said, "Save me, O God, / for the waters have come up to my neck. / I sink in the miry depths, / where there is no foothold. / I have come into the deep waters; / the floods engulf me. / I am worn out calling for help; / my throat is parched. / My eyes fail, / looking for my God" (Ps. 69:1–3).

But Joseph's story demonstrates that *God is not as much interested in our circumstances as our response to circumstances.* Mirroring Joseph's responses can be great training, regardless of your circumstances. God will use your response to firm up your faith and purify your motives.

Joseph Kept a Proper Perspective

In the midst of the normal human feelings resulting from imprisonment, Joseph must have realized the importance of perspective. Perspective depends heavily on focus. It's crucial to avoid becoming introspective, or self-pity will naturally follow. And self-pity also has a natural result—I call it "comfort in sickness" syndrome. Have you ever noticed when you're ill and feeling terrible, it's nice to have someone wait on you? When you need something to drink, or you need some medicine, you like someone to bring it to you. When you want the TV turned on or off, someone becomes your remote control. Eventually you almost dread getting well. The attention has been grand. Being sick, perhaps, isn't all that bad. Your perspective has moved inward.

So it is with some who find themselves in life's prisons. Self-pity takes hold and before long they're not sure they want out. They're getting lots of attention and sympathy. The more they get, the more they want. Rather than finding a way out of the prison of adversity, they snuggle down in the corner of their cell, waiting for the next kind soul to come and minister to them.

Joseph probably would not have received that kind of attention in prison, but he could easily have fallen into the trap of desiring it. He had already bounced back from one devastating blow, only to find himself abandoned, doomed, and forgotten again. But Joseph kept his perspective. He kept his eyes on the God who controls every circumstance. As

Paul, Joseph could say, "I have learned to be content whatever the circumstances. I know what it is to be in need, and I know what it is to have plenty. I have learned the secret of being content in any and every situation, whether well fed or hungry, whether living in plenty or in want. I can do everything through him who gives me strength" (Phil. 4:11–13).

In your present situation, how is your perspective? Has it become inwardly directed? Or are you able to trust God's sovereignty in every situation? Are you a little mad at God? Then you need to heed Isaiah's warning: "Woe to him who quarrels with his Maker, / to him who is but a potsherd among the potsherds on the ground. / Does the clay say to the potter, / 'What are you making?' / Does your work say, 'He has no hands'?" (Isa. 45:9). Be careful, lest in the furnace of your trial, you find yourself striving with God's sovereignty.

Joseph Maintained a Proper Priority

If Joseph had succumbed to his desperate situation, and begun focusing inwardly, he would have lost track of God, and also of the people around him. Prison experiences often stifle your concern for others. This was not the case with Joseph. Even in the midst of adversity, he reached out to help others. As a result, the Bible tells us, "The warden put Joseph in charge of all those held in the prison, and he was made responsible for all that was done there. The warden paid no attention to anything under Joseph's care, because the LORD was with Joseph and gave him success in whatever he did" (Gen. 39:22–23).

During his imprisonment, Joseph met two men who had been trusted officials of Pharaoh's court. The chief cupbearer had the responsibility to taste all the food and drink before Pharaoh ate any meal. If he lived, the Pharaoh felt free to enjoy the meal; if he died . . . oh well, time for another cupbearer. The baker cooked food for his sovereign. Scripture doesn't tell us why they were in prison—only that they became coinmates with Joseph. Whatever happened, it must have been extremely serious to have both of these trusted members of the court imprisoned.

It would have been easy for Joseph to think that "it serves them right—if I'm here, I'm glad they're here too." Instead, Joseph gave himself away in ministry to them. First, he interpreted their dreams as God gave him insight. For the cupbearer, it would be the good news of eventual release. For the chief baker, however, it would be news of ultimate execution. Joseph's ministry to each man was characterized by openness and honesty.

Joseph focused on others' needs before his own. He realized that in giving ourselves away, we actually find ourselves. The greatest gift any of us can give is not money or things, but ourselves.

Joseph Experienced a Perfect Peace

Even in Joseph's incarceration, Scripture gives no indication of bitterness, resentment, or worry about himself. Though he did not have Scripture to read at that point, he understood what would be a spiritual principle of the New Testament. "Do not be anxious about anything, but in everything, by prayer and petition, with thanksgiving, present your requests to God. And the peace of God, which transcends all understanding, will guard your hearts and your minds in Christ Jesus" (Phil. 4:6–7).

Joseph must have understood that worry can be debilitating. Instead, he made his requests known to God. Obviously, he wanted to be released from prison. In his daily prayers he probably asked God for deliverance. But even in the midst of continued difficult circumstances, peace pervaded his life. Joseph knew that, even in his prison experience, God was accomplishing His purpose.

Yet even with this peace, we find Joseph requesting the help of another to gain release. Genesis 40:14 tells us Joseph asked the cupbearer to remember him and his kindness by mentioning his situation to Pharaoh. Like any of us, he wanted out. Asking others for help is perfectly acceptable. They may be the instruments God will use to release us from imprisonment. However, the final deliverance will be accomplished by God Himself. Joseph had peace even when the chief cupbearer failed to remember him.

Joseph didn't have the luxury of reading Philippians 4:6–7, yet he undoubtedly had the "peace of God." Because Joseph was at peace with his Creator by being in right relationship with Him, and was obedient to God's leadership in his life, he was able to experience the peace of God.

Joseph Exhibited a Positive Attitude

If Joseph had gotten angry or frustrated, we would have understood. Yet we find no such evidence. He maintained the posture of serving faithfully, keeping his eyes on God and remaining in perfect peace. How liberating that choice proved to be, for anger and frustration cripple us emotionally and spiritually.

I'm convinced that ninety percent of how we feel is determined by our attitudes. Circumstances may change, but attitude makes or breaks our ability to cope and to have a positive impact on our environment.

Dick Woodward is one of the greatest Bible teachers I know. Chuck Colson has said that he may be one of the finest Bible teachers in all of America. Yet Dick cannot move from his neck down.

Several years ago, Dick pastored a church in the Virginia Beach area. His practical, application-oriented Bible teaching began to draw people by the hundreds. In addition, Dick started a men's Bible study at the stadium where the Norfolk Tides (AAA minor league team) regularly played. Men swarmed to the study, and hundreds came to know Christ.

The principles he taught on *Maximizing Your Marriage* also became a flagship of Dick's ministry. Couple after couple were reunited through his biblical teaching. Some had been divorced and came back together. Others were on the verge of a divorce tragedy. Still others were seeing the seams of their holy matrimony strained to the point of rupture.

In the midst of all that, Dick became ill. A degenerative condition in his spine began to take its toll. But Dick kept teaching and preaching. The time came when he could only preach from a wheelchair. And the crowds kept coming. Now Dick lies in a bed every day, unable to do his own typing or writing. Yet he teaches every day from his bedside and is the guest preacher on a worldwide radio broadcast.

I've never seen Dick but what a smile has been on his face, and his incredible wife Ginny has been smiling by his side. When I ask him how he's doing, he always responds, "Much better than I deserve." In any discussion, he will make a point to talk about God's goodness and grace and how faithful He is. Dick always reminds me that God best uses "broken vessels."

How are you doing in your situation? Are you like Dick, making the best of the circumstances in which you find yourself? Your attitude will greatly determine the outcome of your present circumstances. And your attitude will be determined by whether you see your circumstances through the lens of God's faithfulness, or you see God's faithfulness through the lens of your circumstances. Your choice will make all the difference.

Joseph Exuded a Patient Demeanor

Joseph patiently waited for the Lord's deliverance. We find patience so difficult. In our instant society of microwave ovens, microchip computers, and millisecond transmission of information, we don't like to wait. We want instant gratification. We look for patience in a gift-wrapped package that God drops in our laps at the mere asking. Unfortunately, patience is born and refined in the crucible of difficult circumstances.

Even as I write this book, I'm having to exercise the faith of dealing with the prison of pain. Unexpectedly, I suffered a severe cervical spinal injury. The pain was so excruciating, the hospital staff couldn't even get me into the MRI until they had significantly sedated me. The MRI showed significant damage at three major points in the cervical area. The orthopedic surgeon's assistant later told me, "Bob, your neck is a wreck." He said there was hardly any way I could avoid surgery.

Because of the swelling of injured nerve bundles, the only way I could relieve the pain was to use a strong prescribed narcotic and to lie on bags of ice. Sleep, what little there was, came only by sitting in a reclining chair.

Approximately forty-eight hours from the onset of the injury, doctors estimated that I lost about eighty percent of the strength in my left arm. Three fingers on my left hand totally lost feeling. Even the slightest movements would send pain waves hurtling down my left side and shoulder. To add insult to injury, physicians said I had to step away completely from my work (which I love), and begin to wear a neck brace . . . twenty-four hours a day for five-and-a-half weeks.

About halfway through that experience, I found myself sitting on the screened-in porch behind our home. The day was cold and blustery, but I was committed to being outside, just for a change of scenery. Suddenly a bird landed on the railing and began to sing. On that cold, rainy day, I couldn't believe anything had a reason to sing. I wanted to shoot that bird! But he continued to warble, and I had no choice but to listen.

The next day found me on the porch again, but this time the atmosphere was bright, sunny, and warm. As I sat, being tempted to feel sorry for myself, suddenly the bird (at least it looked like the same one) returned. And he was singing again! Where was that shotgun?

Then an amazing truth hit me head on: the bird sang in the cold rain as well as the sunny warmth. His song was not altered by outward circumstances, but it was held constant by an internal condition. It was as though God quietly said to me, "You've got the same choice, Bob. You will either let external circumstances mold your attitude, or your attitude will rise above external circumstances. You choose!"

That day proved to be a significant turning point in my attitude and outlook. Today, three months later, through the prayers of God's people and the faithfulness of God's grace, I have been able to avoid surgery and am well on the road to recovery. But even had I not, the lesson would have remained the same.

While waiting may not be one of our strong suits, Scripture tells us it is one of the endearing characteristics of the man or woman who follows God. The writer of Proverbs said, "Man's wisdom gives him patience" (Prov. 19:11). The psalmist wrote, "Wait for the LORD; / be strong and take heart / and wait for the LORD" (Ps. 27:14). Isaiah said, "Yet the LORD longs to be gracious to you; / he rises to show you compassion. / For the LORD is a God of justice. / Blessed are all who wait for him!" (Isa. 30:18).

Joseph realized four great principles of patiently waiting for God's move in the midst of trials:

1. God's timing will always show our inadequacy in an impossible situation. Joseph could do nothing to extricate himself from his cell. The possibility of freedom seemed nonexistent. It is in these very times that God moves. God's confidence begins at the end of self-confidence.

2. God is adequate for every circumstance and situation. God's timing will always be such that it will show His adequacy in impossible situations. God has never promised to remove all the obstacles, but instead to give us what is needed to cope with them. To the apostle Paul, He never promised to remove the problems, but instead said, "My grace is sufficient for you" (2 Cor. 12:9).

3. God's timing will always be such that He will get the greatest glory. This was beautifully illustrated when Jesus' dear friend Lazarus lay dying. Mary and Martha, his sisters, urgently sent for Christ with the message, "Lord, the one you love is sick" (John 11:3). Our immediate expectation would be that Jesus would hurry to Bethany to heal His friend. Instead, Jesus delayed two more days. Why? Jesus Himself gave the answer: "This sickness will not end in death. No, it is for God's glory so that God's Son may be glorified through it" (John 11:4). Perhaps you are waiting for God to move, but if He were to do so immediately, you or someone else would receive the glory. He will wait until He knows His name will be glorified in the solution. Be patient.

4. *What's impossible to us isn't impossible to God.* There's no prison door that God can't open. He is the Master escape artist. And He doesn't need your help. All He needs is your cooperation and submission. There is always a danger that you presume God is much too small. If you find yourself imprisoned, you feel that He must be limited as well. But God is not limited to our dimensions or circumstances. He reigns supreme. He is able.

Consider the story of Peter's imprisonment in Acts 12. By all accounts, things looked pretty bad, as though there were really no hope for Peter. He was kept in prison with greater than normal security. The circumstances drove the church to pray earnestly and constantly for Peter. The whole church in Jerusalem took the issue of Peter's arrest and imprisonment as a problem only God could solve. Yet God allowed Peter to stay in prison for many days.

Think about the arrangement in the prison. Peter was sleeping between two soldiers to whom he was bound by chains—there was nothing Peter could do to save himself. There was nothing the church could do by force or by stealth to obtain his escape.

The death of James only stirred them into a deeper earnestness in their petition to God for Peter's life. They prayed not only for Peter's safety and release, but they prayed that, if Peter was released, it would crush and embarrass Herod's planned persecution of the Church. They prayed, and they waited. Their prayers were answered the evening before Herod was planning to sentence Peter. Herod had taken all earthly measures to insure that Peter would indeed die. God, however, had another plan.

In this destitute situation, when all hope seemed lost, when no human effort that the church could have organized would have been successful, when no one human being could have taken the credit, God made His presence known. God was in charge of the timing, and that same God remains in charge of the timing of His intervention in human events.

Peter was asleep in the prison. Amazing isn't it? He was asleep in the grasp of, and literally "between," the enemy. God gave him rest, even though Peter was not expecting to be rescued. He slept—with just a sunrise between him and death—sitting behind locked prison doors with armed guards, and shackled on the hard floor with the heavy weight of metal chains linking him between two armed soldiers. And then, God's unmistakable power and presence moved in.

What a scene it must have been. No computerized virtual reality program could simulate the shock and amazement received by the senses of those who were in the prison that night. The sights and sounds were nothing Hollywood could produce because they were not of this world. Indeed, they were from an entirely other realm than anything the guards, or we, have ever witnessed.

Peter awoke. His first thoughts must have been, "I must be dreaming." In the foggy state of consciousness between sleeping and awaking, Peter must have been taken aback and sensed a strange familiarity as it all began to unfold around him. He probably wondered when it was that he'd felt before this same kind of "presence." Then he would have remembered it was on the night that Christ was transfigured on the mountaintop. What a long time ago that must have seemed, and how ironic that he was feeling this way in the prison.

But he was not simply remembering—he was experiencing something new. He thought he dreamed that light was shining into the prison. He sensed that a messenger was sent from God to release him from the prison. The soldiers around him were either rendered unconscious or immobilized with fear. Either way, they were not going to move about any time soon. The messenger touched Peter on the side; he felt pain and was startled. Then the silence was shattered by the clanging sound made as the iron chains that bound Peter's wrists hit the stone floor of the prison. It was the sweet sound of freedom.

Peter quickly did as he was told: he dressed and put on his sandals. Then he followed God's messenger out the door of the prison, past the place where one guard watched, and then another. Yet they went undetected, all the way through the heavy iron gates. They were in the street now. They walked some distance, perhaps a block or so, and after turning around, Peter didn't see the one who had led him out—Peter was alone in the street. But more importantly, he was free. He was out of danger and no longer needed protection.

He wondered again if he were dreaming. Too many things had happened at once. He felt confused. Was he sleeping? No. He realized he had all of his faculties. The truth of what had happened was too real to doubt any more. It was then that he was certain of what had happened: God had delivered him. God had given an angel orders to come on a special mission to earth for one purpose: to release Peter from the prison.

There are no prison doors God cannot open. If you find yourself imprisoned in what seems like hopeless circumstances, think about Peter's release. First, the "lights came on," just as God will, if we ask, bring us the light of understanding and the awakening of our conscience. Then the chains of bondage fall off as we renew our will and align it with God's will. We then must be prepared, with God's guidance, to work our way through the difficulties that must inevitably be confronted, just as Peter had to work his way past the guards and the gate. At the end of it all, the final gate will open before us and we will be made free again.

Chuck Swindoll, president of Dallas Theological Seminary, said, "We are all faced with innumerable opportunities brilliantly disguised as impossible situations."

Just remember, nothing is impossible with God. With His divine intervention, no prison cell will ever hold you. But like Joseph, you need God to release you from your prison of pressure. As you wait for His timing, allow Him to empower you to deal with the circumstances in which you find yourself. Your circumstances will never make or break you. Instead, you will make or break your circumstances. Remember—when the pressure is on, what's inside will inevitably come out.

Putting Yourself in the Refiner's Hands

1. Recall some ways in which people find themselves "imprisoned" in life. Have you known anyone imprisoned by some of these things? Are you imprisoned by some of these things?
2. How did Joseph respond to his imprisonment? Imagine yourself in his shoes. How do you think you would have responded?
3. Why is it so easy for your perspective to become self-centered in the midst of adversity? How do you prevent this?

4. What was Joseph's view of God in the midst of adversity? What do you normally find yours to be? If there is a difference, what do you think is the reason?
5. We looked at some principles of waiting found in Joseph's life. Practically apply these three principles to your most recent experience of waiting.

EIGHT

Cooling Is Just as Important as Heating

IN SMELTING AND FORGING, THE COOLING process is as important as the heating process. Metallurgists have discovered that changes occur in the metal itself during the cool-down or waiting period. If the cool-down is too fast, it can cause microscopic cracks in the metal that will inevitably lead to fatigue . . . and ultimately to disaster.

Several methods are used to insure that the cooling process actually aids in the strengthening of the metal:

- The metal is placed in a quenching bath, and then, when an appropriate temperature is reached, it is allowed to cool slowly in the air.
- The metal is removed from the quenching bath and then dropped into a constant-temperature bath until it attains uniform temperature throughout. It is then allowed to cool in the air until it reaches room temperature.
- The metal is placed in constant-temperature salt baths to insure structural uniformity in the cooling process.

Regardless of the method chosen, waiting becomes an essential so that the metal remains strong and productive to accomplish its ultimate end use.

We, too, go through times of waiting—cool-down periods. And in those times, the Great Refiner strives to build into our lives the qualities that will fit us most effectively for the ultimate use He has in mind. Waiting becomes an inescapable segment of the process. It is essential that you and I understand that God is every bit as interested in the process through which He takes us as He is in the product He's forming us into.

Waiting Rooms

Have you ever noticed that rooms speak for themselves?

Walk into a freshly decorated nursery, and the room speaks of joy and excitement. On a cold winter evening, enter a cozy den, with a large fire playing percussion in the fireplace, and shadows dancing in syncopated rhythm on the walls and ceiling. The room invites you to sit down and succumb to its atmosphere. Or walk into a festive holiday dining room. Plates at each chair await a sumptuous feast. Friendly voices and warm laughter drift from down the hall. The room sings the theme of celebration and reunion.

Other rooms aren't nearly so inviting—for example, waiting rooms.

David Baxter knows all about waiting rooms. He married his high school sweetheart in 1990, and they had three sons, all of whom had unique medical problems. The first was diagnosed with hydrocephalus, commonly called "water on the brain." The second was born prematurely and has hearing and speech difficulties. The third had difficulty breathing at birth and spent two weeks in a neonatal intensive care unit.

David has seen plenty of waiting rooms in medical institutions. But he also knows about waiting rooms in life. Sensing God's call to church planting, David accepted a position in California. But as plans unfolded for his church start, the sponsoring church's support evaporated. Funding never materialized. David was put "on hold" in God's waiting room.

During this "cool-down" period, his family went to Texas, and David continued to work for several months, trying to see what God was doing. Staff at the Southern Baptist Convention's North American Mission Board tried to help him go to some other locations, but since there was no clear sense of God's leadership, David chose to wait.

One month passed. Then two. Then three . . . When five months had dragged by, David wondered if God had forgotten about him. Suddenly, though, at the end of six months, a door of opportunity swung open. The Florida Baptist Convention invited him to plant a new church in the Orlando area. God hadn't forgotten. He was just allowing his "metal" to become ready for its ultimate use.

Waiting Isn't Easy

You see, for all of us, life brings many experiences that develop into "waiting rooms."

Maybe you're waiting to launch into a new arena of education. Or maybe you've completed your formal education and are waiting for employment. Maybe you're waiting to have children, or at the other end of the spectrum, maybe you're waiting for them to leave home. Maybe you're waiting for a long-anticipated trip. Or maybe you're just waiting to die.

It's almost impossible for a person not to be waiting for something. And waiting is never easy. I'm sure it's always been difficult, but I truly believe our culture has made it even harder. We live in a society that has ready-made frozen dinners and instant potatoes. Our phones are touch-tone and mobile, so we can do two things at once. Our ovens are microwaves. Our information is generated on a computer screen at the touch of a keyboard. Our culture demands instant gratification and immediate success.

Yet all of us face times when God seems to hit the "pause" button on our lives, and He invites—and sometimes forces—us to accept a posture of waiting. Joseph's story provides critical insight for handling those times. He lived in a "waiting room." Imprisoned on false charges, his deliverance didn't come quickly.

As we noted in the previous chapter, Joseph met the Pharaoh's chief baker and cupbearer in prison, and he interpreted their dreams. For the cupbearer, there was good news of release and restoration. For the chief baker, there was no good news at all, as his dream foretold his execution. Joseph requested that, when he was released from jail, the cupbearer would speak to Pharaoh on his behalf (Gen. 40:14). But the cupbearer forgot his imprisoned friend, and Joseph's life continued in a low-altitude holding pattern for two years. Sometimes he surely felt he was running out of fuel.

Then suddenly the holding pattern was interrupted. The day probably began similar to every other day in prison. Just another day in the dungeon. Forgotten. Alone. Wasted. But the normal doldrums were jolted by a dilemma. Pharaoh had a couple of dreams: seven sickly, skinny cows devoured seven fat cows, and then seven scorched and dry ears of grain swallowed up seven picture-perfect ears of grain.

Pharaoh's magicians and counselors simply couldn't interpret these strange dreams. Then suddenly the cupbearer remembered Joseph, and he told Pharaoh about the young man in jail who had successfully deciphered his and the baker's dreams.

Joseph was immediately summoned, and he rocketed from the pit to the pinnacle in one quick step. The time of waiting in the stone-cold dungeon had finally expired. He had been in Egypt for thirteen years. His arduous ordeal had put him to the test, and he had passed with flying colors.

Biblical Principles for Life's Waiting Periods

Though Joseph was not as fortunate as we are in having God's counsel revealed through the Bible, he seemed to sense intuitively principles for godly living. His principles for coping with the rigors of waiting are still valid today.

1. Wait alertly. During waiting periods, we should be especially sensitive to God's intentions and actions. Wisdom herself relates, "Blessed is the man who listens to me, / watching daily at my doors, / waiting at my doorway" (Prov. 8:34). If you think waiting is a passive endeavor, you're wrong. You can't effectively wait by simply sitting on your hands—you must be alertly tuned to God.

You see, God often uses cool-downs and waiting rooms to prepare us for something we will encounter later in life. If we are docilely folding our hands and enduring these faith-stretching times, we are wasting valuable time. Scripture suggests we should listen and watch. This requires active concentration and attention.

In my own waiting rooms, I've found help in asking two questions:

- Is God trying to teach me something during this time of waiting?
- Is God trying to change something specific in my life during this time of waiting?

These two questions often have brought me face-to-face with a fresh perspective, regardless of whether I wanted it at the time. Before this became my reality, I wasted time in many waiting rooms. I have often been distracted by the superficial and missed the supernatural. God promises to direct our lives and give counsel. That promise doesn't cease to exist just because we're waiting.

Joseph apparently knew how to wait with his spiritual ears straining to pick up even the faintest whisper of God's voice. As a result, his waiting room became a training ground which molded him to become more like his God. When we follow Joseph's example, we will find that God will develop and refresh our sensitivity to Him. When things are going well, we seem to have little need for the Father's care. On the other hand, when we are waiting, we become keenly aware of our need.

It's also true, however, that at such times our adversary moves to undermine us with whispers of doubt. God warns us to "be self-controlled and alert. Your enemy the devil prowls around like a roaring lion looking for someone to devour. Resist him, standing firm in the faith" (1 Pet. 5:8–9). Notice, this is one imperative where we are responsible for the action. We have the freedom to choose whether we will be alert or dulled. We either draw close to the Lord, or we drift from Him. We either resist the devil's attacks of doubt, anger, and frustration, or we surrender a beachhead in our lives. Whatever the outcome, it will directly result from our choice.

2. *Wait expectantly.* Have you ever waited for something you really wanted? I have. As days and weeks passed without seeing fulfillment, my expectancy began to dwindle. I questioned whether the dream would ever materialize.

Then I discovered what the psalmist wrote: "I wait for the LORD, my soul waits, / and in his word I put my hope. / My soul waits for the Lord / more than watchmen wait for the morning" (Ps. 130:5–6). The biblical writer put his hope in God's Word. I had to admit that, as I had waited, my commitment to reading and internalizing Scripture had waned. The psalmist's experience was different. He expected God to fulfill His Word, even more than a watchman expects to see the sun rise in the morning.

Determining that sunrise was a fairly trustworthy occurrence, I went back to basics: either I trusted God and His Word, or I didn't. That led me to two questions:

- What does this kind of trust entail? Scripture doesn't lightly suggest that we should put our hope in God and His Word. This is more than wistful longing. The Bible uses the word *hope* to refer to the solid expectation of grace and deliverance. In Hebrews 11:1 we read: "Faith is being sure of what we hope for and certain of what we do not see." Living with that type of faith gives absolute assurance, regardless of circumstances. Biblical hope is the most solid ground on which to stand. It is the conviction that God will do as He says.
- Where do we get that type of hope? Scripture tells us, "For everything that was written in the past was written to teach

> us, so that through endurance and the encouragement of the Scriptures we might have hope" (Rom. 15:4).

Joseph didn't have the advantage of reading God's Word, but we do. When circumstances require patient endurance, the Bible is the best source of encouragement and hope. God's faithfulness is spelled out on every page. The process of reading and applying the lessons recorded there provides the raw material that rebuilds and restores hope.

In the Old Testament, we read, of course, of Joseph. But we also meet Noah, who obediently built a big boat, preparing for a promised flood in a land where it had never rained. We become acquainted with Abraham. God told this man he would have a son, and then fulfilled the promise years later, when Abraham and his wife were both past childbearing years. We meet a young man named David, anointed to be king of Israel. Then God allowed him to wander for years in the wilderness, living as a fugitive, before He finally gave David the promised throne.

In the New Testament, we meet Anna and Simeon, who waited their entire lifetimes to see the Messiah, and when they were old, God granted their desire. We see Mary and Martha, who asked Jesus to come and heal their brother. Jesus came, but only after their brother had died. Their frustration is evident, but then they had cause to rejoice when Jesus called their brother forth from the grave. We see Jesus after His resurrection, giving His followers the task of taking the good news of salvation to the entire world. But first, He says, they must wait until God gives them the gift of the Holy Spirit.

The same God asks us to wait. And from the examples recorded in His Word, we learn that waiting is part of His plan for preparing His people. We see His purpose, and we come to accept that His faithfulness is primary, and our circumstances are secondary.

When we are in the midst of waiting, we can honestly say, "I know that God has a reason for this and He will bring me through." Then we are waiting expectantly. Isaiah 40:31 promises, "But they that *wait* upon the LORD shall renew their strength; they shall mount up with wings as eagles; they shall run, and not be weary; and they shall walk, and not faint" (KJV, italics added). As we shift focus from the hope that "things will work out" to the "God who works all things out," we will know internal renewal. Our spirits will soar as if they had the wings of eagles.

That sounds almost poetic, doesn't it? But before you start feeling all cozy and warm, let's consider how eagles learn to soar. It's not an easy or enjoyable process.

Mother Eagle lines her nest with soft animal fur and grass. As the newly hatched babies begin to mature, they nestle in a soft and cozy home. Before long, though, they begin to flex their muscles, and Mother realizes her babies have advanced to a new stage of development. She wisely begins to rip away the soft lining. What had been a nice lounging area becomes a devilish tangle of thorns, broken sticks, and branches. The lack of comfort fosters the desire to go on to the next stage.

Then Mom grabs an eaglet in her talons and soars to the heights. Amazing things must cross this little bird's mind as he gets a bird's-eye view from such altitudes. He's just learning to enjoy the ride when suddenly, he feels Mom's talons loosen, and he plummets toward the earth. Can you imagine the sheer panic? Just when he loses all hope of rescue, Mom swoops under him, catching him on her powerful shoulders. The baby's heartbeat gradually slows. Surely they must be headed back to the nest. But again, Mom soars high in the air. She dips her shoulder and the eaglet falls.

After several of these wild experiments, the little bird's wings begin to function. The air currents course over their leading edge. As the strong feathered armatures catch the moving air, the eaglet begins to hold himself aloft. Soon he isn't just flying—he's soaring.

That's how God treats you and me. It doesn't mean He doesn't love us—it means He loves us enough to create an environment that will require us to mature. Sometimes He allows us to fall through the unknown. He doesn't respond as quickly as we would like, and sometimes His deliverance isn't a once-for-all experience. We will again find ourselves waiting for His rescue. All the while, He is forcing us to use our spiritual wings. Then, even in the midst of waiting, we will know His restoration.

Joseph waited expectantly. Because of God's promise and his own past experience, he expected deliverance. And it became reality.

3. *Wait quietly and patiently.* My father-in-law knew me well. A few years ago he purchased a plaque for my study. On it was what I call the American prayer: "Lord grant me patience . . . and grant it to me now!"

Many of us have trouble being quiet and patient. Yet these are critical ingredients of effective waiting.

Scripture tells us, "The LORD is good to those whose hope is in him, / to the one who seeks him; / it is good to wait quietly / for the salvation of the LORD" (Lam. 3:25–26).

Have you ever noticed how hard it is for people to wait quietly? Just watch some time when motorists have to wait through two or three changes of a traffic signal. Or consider how we complain vehemently when we're put on hold on the telephone.

We're really not that much different than people throughout the ages. Take the nation of Israel, for instance. When God led His people into the Promised Land, He gave them a strange strategy for conquering Jericho. They were to march around the city once daily for six days. On the seventh day they were to march around seven times, sound the trumpets and shout, and the walls would tumble down. But God added one crucial requirement—the people were instructed not to talk at all during those seven days.

I think I have an idea why God issued such a mandate. Prior to that time, when God moved in a miraculous way to deliver them, the Israelites were thankful—for a few hours, days, or weeks. Then some new type of trial would come, and they would quickly forget how God had provided in the recent past. Soon you would hear, "Murmur, murmur, murmur, murmur . . . complain, complain, complain." Again and again, God moved on their behalf, meeting their needs in a most incredible and unexpected way. Yet somehow it never seemed to sink in.

I believe God asked the children of Israel to march quietly around Jericho, because He knew if they talked, they'd end up complaining and murmuring. If we don't practice that same kind of discipline in controlling our tongues, we can easily fall into the same trap. We must put a guard at our lips, because that staunch sentinel allows us to hear God more clearly. How many times have you and I missed God's voice because we were too busy complaining about the present situation? We should spend more time recalling how God has provided for us in the past and less time murmuring about our present circumstances. This is true even when the present circumstances rage like a hurricane around us.

While living in Florida, I became fascinated with hurricanes. I well remember when a hurricane called "David" was racing toward the coast of Fort Lauderdale. Warnings blanketed our city, and everyone began preparing for potential disaster. People stocked up on every commodity that would be needed should the worst occur. Glass windows were taped and braced to withstand the coming winds.

As the winds began to make the trees outside of our home dance like marionettes, I tuned in to the weather reports. The announcer explained that, though winds may race over a hundred miles per hour along the edge of the hurricane, the center, or the "eye," is very calm—so peaceful, in fact, that a plane can fly around inside it for some time with no turbulence.

I thought about how God is like the center of a hurricane. Though life may be swirling at an incredible pace, God's presence can bring an unearthly quietness. It is only in spending time with Him that the frantic winds of life become still. Have you tried letting Him be the eye of your storm?

Along with quiet waiting, we must wait patiently. Again the biblical writer instructs us to come "be still before the LORD and wait patiently for him" (Ps. 37:7).

Patience, unfortunately, is a commodity in short supply. The word most often used in Scripture for *patience* is a word that means "to abide under." It means that we are unwilling to surrender and collapse when under trying circumstances. This "abiding under" can have both a passive and active quality.

The active quality as used in Scripture indicates pressing on despite obstacles, an active determination not to give in—not to falter from exhaustion or difficulty. This is what the writer of Hebrews meant when he said, "Let us run with perseverance the race marked out for us. Let us fix our eyes on Jesus, the author and perfecter of our faith" (12:1–2). The Scripture pictures a distance runner, not a sprinter. Even when his body cries out from fatigue, his mind does not give in. He instructs his body to keep running. That's how it is with the race of life. God calls us to press on.

Once we have done all that we can, we must also trust God to accomplish His purposes. This more passive posture is often referred to as endurance. Romans 12:12 tells us, "Be joyful in hope, patient in affliction, faithful in prayer." Paul uses it also in 2 Timothy when he writes, "Therefore I endure everything for the sake of the elect, that they too may obtain the salvation that is in Christ Jesus, with eternal glory. . . . if we endure, we will also reign with him" (2:10–12).

In waiting patiently, both the active and passive elements are involved. And they are always directed toward a purpose, as revealed in James 1:2–4: "Consider it pure joy, my brothers, whenever you face trials of many kinds, because you know that the testing of your faith develops perseverance. Perseverance must finish its work so that you may be mature and complete, not lacking anything."

Waiting, both actively and passively, has its own reward—maturity. And that maturity, in turn, equips us to handle everything that may come our way.

This is, indeed, what was happening in Joseph's life. Scripture gives no indication that he murmured and complained. Though it seemed he had been forgotten, he was quiet. Though things weren't on his timetable, he was patient. Though at times circumstances probably seemed unbearable, he was unwilling to surrender and collapse under them.

4. *Wait realistically.* God is never in a hurry. Though we work on a limited timetable, God works from and toward eternity. When God is in the process of making His man or woman, He will take every bit of time needed to make that person the best he or she can be. He is not the author of shortcuts.

If you find yourself waiting, you must determine what you really want to be. Remember, an oak tree takes a hundred years to grow to maturity. On the other hand, a flower requires only a few months. The difference is that one stands the test of time and the other, though beautiful for a brief period, withers and dies. It's the same in the spiritual realm. If you are to develop a character that will endure, you must be willing for God to take the time to accomplish that end. Nothing that lasts happens quickly.

Paul said it eloquently: "Being confident of this, that he who began a good work in you will carry it on to completion" (Phil. 1:6).

5. *Wait cautiously.* One final word about waiting. As we've noted previously, when the delay lengthens, the natural instinct is to complain. "Where is God? Doesn't He have my best interest at heart? Doesn't He know time is passing rapidly? All the good opportunities are passing me by."

At that point, we are potentially in great danger. We have a tendency to strive with sovereignty.

Striving with Sovereignty

The Israelites had this problem. During their Babylonian captivity, they waited for God to send a deliverer. They were convinced He would be a strong Jewish firebrand. He would ride a white stallion and lead the Jews to victory over Babylonian domination.

That isn't how God chose to work. Years of captivity passed. Finally God raised up one to be the deliverer (literally "the messiah"). He was Cyrus, a Gentile king. He didn't even believe in God, yet he became His chosen instrument. That wasn't what the Jewish people expected, but it was God's plan.

God used the prophet Isaiah to bring a word of caution to the people of that day and of our own time—to those who seek to work out their own way rather than submitting to God's strategy. Repeatedly He says, "I am the Lord, and there is no other." He states His right to work out His sovereign plan in the lives of His people. It is in that context that He states, "Woe to him who quarrels with his Maker . . . / Does the clay say to the potter, / 'What are you making?'" (Isa. 45:9).

Yet many people refuse to heed the warning, and they test God's plan in two ways:

1. They become totally passive in their relationship with Him. They don't give Him much attention. They slack off on prayer. They reduce the time spent in His Word, reading the Bible for mileage more than content. When they come across something relevant, they think about how it applies to everybody else. Their desire to be with God's people also diminishes.

2. They engage in active rebellion. Spiritually, they shake their fists in God's face. They become angry at His action, or more often than not, His seeming inaction.

Looking for "Plan B"

Anyone who succumbs to either of those two attitudes will tend to develop his own plan for deliverance. Like the

Jewish people Isaiah addressed, we all want a dramatic answer. We have not only the method but, quite often, the timetable. And yet God usually refuses to work according to either. And so we continue to wait. I've noticed three interesting tendencies about people who are testing God in their waiting.

1. *We tend to look to God as a last resort rather than a first source.* Perhaps it's self-confidence. Perhaps it's pride. Perhaps it's pure stubbornness. Whatever the cause, too often we strike out on our own, feeling we're equal to anything, and painfully discovering we're not. Sometimes we lapse into a "between-a-rock-and-hard-place" faith. We turn to God only when there seems to be no other way out. We need to approach the Father on the front end. He knows our every need before we even breathe it, so why do we keep it from Him so long? We waste a lot of time that could be put to much better use if we just went to Him, seeking His Word and counsel when life's challenges begin.

2. *We desire deliverance by our own timetable and method rather than His.* A strong-willed two-year-old can drive you crazy with his "I-can-do-it-myself" mentality. Yet we often reflect that posture in our spiritual lives. We get into the savior business. We become our own god. We assume we know best how to handle our various circumstances. We succumb to an age of self-sufficiency, launching out on our own without God's schedule or map. Scripture clearly tells us that, when He delivered His people, it was always in His time and in His way.

3. *We border on preferring not to have an answer if God's answer doesn't agree with ours.* This is perhaps the most dangerous tendency of all, for it brings God's discipline.

Like a good parent, He will lovingly do what He must to direct our lives as He determines best.

Scripture pulls no punches when it warns us about striving with our Maker. So, if you find yourself in that position, what should you do? First of all, get back to the basics.

When the late Vince Lombardi, the successful coach of the Green Bay Packers, saw his team struggling, he faced the issue up-front. He said any group of naturally-talented athletes could win more games than they lost. The key was concentrating on the fundamentals. Following the loss of a close game, Lombardi called a special Monday meeting. Standing before the players, he declared, "Men, we need to review the fundamentals of the game." Holding a football above his head, he continued, "This is a football."

When we are bucking God's plan, we must return to the fundamentals. Regardless of how you feel about it, get back into regular Bible study. Even if you don't feel much like praying, spend time clearly communicating with your Father. And be honest. Don't try to cover up your real attitudes, like so many do. If they pray at all, they pray as though nothing were really wrong. But God looks at our motivations and our intentions. He doesn't just hear what we say. Perhaps you might pray something like this:

> *Heavenly Father, right now I'm not happy with the way things are. I'm frustrated with circumstances. Sometimes it seems as though You are a million miles away. Today I'm not sure that I love you or myself. I don't want to be with other Christians. My hunger for your Word is all but nonexistent. And honestly, I'm angry. But Lord, I know this is not the way I should be. I admit that it is wrong. I ask You to change these attitudes. Restore the joy of my salvation. Create in my heart a hunger for Your Word, Your people, and You, Yourself. By faith, I thank You that You are already working in my heart to bring about these changes.*

Be ready. Having asked in faith, things will change. Be sure your attitude is ready to let the changes take effect. You'll be glad you did.

A Time to Wait and a Time to Act

We have looked at some helpful guidelines on how to deal with life's waiting rooms. In the midst of waiting, we are never without hope. If you are waiting for something right now, remember that nothing is impossible with God. When I find myself waiting, I am always reminded of the motto of the U.S. Army Corps of Engineers: *"The difficult we do immediately; the impossible takes a little longer."*

I'm not sure about the army engineers, but I've seen God do the impossible over and over again. Though you may be disappointed as you stand in your time of waiting, remember that God can change your disappointments into His appointments.

Don't be lulled into inactivity and insensitivity. As important as it is to wait appropriately, it is just as important not to be always waiting for something. Many people are wasting a lot of their lives sitting around waiting when God would have them actively stepping out in faith. They simply endure the present while waiting for the future. They wait for an elusive tomorrow without realizing the importance of today. There comes a time when we must be sure we are not living in yesterday, for it is gone—nor in tomorrow, for it may never come. In reality, we find ourselves living "in the meantime." We must honestly evaluate where we are in the present.

If God has you in a time of waiting, be sure to wait effectively. But if the time of waiting is drawing to a conclusion, be sure you are not numbed into inactivity. Be willing to step out in the boldness of faith. Remember, life's cool-down periods and waiting rooms not only have entrance doors but exit doors as well.

Putting Yourself in the Refiner's Hands

1. Why is waiting such a difficult part of life?
2 In this chapter, what did you learn about waiting by studying the history of the people of Israel?
3. What does it mean to strive with God's sovereignty? How do we do that?
4. After reading and thinking about waiting, if you had to counsel someone who was dealing with waiting, what would you say?

NINE

Stamped with Integrity

THE METAL USED FOR THE FAN BLADE IN United Flight 232 failed because it lacked integrity. It wasn't trustworthy. A small fissure in the metal turned into a fatal flaw.

Different kinds of metal perform different functions:

- Carbon steels are often used in machines, automobile bodies, structural steel for buildings, and ship hulls, down to as small a product as bobby pins.
- Alloy steels are often used for automobile gears and axles, roller skates, and carving knives.
- High-strength low-alloy steels have become extremely useful for automobile parts, thus reducing the weight of the car, as well as for girders which can be made thinner yet with strategic strength to allow additional space within a building.
- Stainless steels retain their strength for long periods at extremely high or low temperatures. Therefore, they are often used to patch or replace broken bones, for kitchens and facilities where food is prepared, and for surgical instruments.

- Tool steels are forged into cutting and shaping parts of power-driven machinery for manufacturing operations in which extra strength, hardness, and resistance to wear are critical.

Yet for all of these types of steel, integrity is essential for their ultimate productivity. The same thing is true in our lives. Integrity is crucial if we are to be used by God as a tool to expand His kingdom in this world.

What Is Integrity?

Integrity is the characteristic that gives people a sense that they can trust you. It allows them to do business with you on the strength of a handshake. It gives them confidence that, when you promise to do something, you'll do it. I put the word *integrity* into the thesaurus of my computer. These are the synonyms it listed: honesty, virtue, honor, morality, principle, uprightness, righteousness, goodness, completeness. You could just as easily add *character* to that list of synonyms.

The word *character* comes from a Greek term describing a marking or engraving instrument used in metal work. It paints a verbal picture of an artist wearing a groove on a metal plate, or etching an identification mark in a valuable metal. According to *Vine's Expository Dictionary of New Testament Words*, for the Greek artisan, a *tupos* was the impression of a seal. It could also be the stamp made by a die. It was a pattern that could be followed. This is the picture that Paul had in mind when he wrote, "Join with others in following my example, brothers, and take note of those who live according to the *pattern* we gave you" (Phil. 3:17, italics added). The pattern he described was the one he taught. But it was also the one he lived, because he was a man of *integrity*.

The marks of character in my life and yours depend on the presence or absence of integrity, for it is the cornerstone for character. It was true for Joseph. As we've detailed the specific events of his life, it's become obvious that he was stamped with integrity. It was the defining characteristic of his life. Even in the midst of extreme temptation and difficulty, he could have echoed the words of Job, who said, "I will not deny my integrity. / I will maintain my righteousness and never let go of it; / my conscience will not reproach me as long as I live" (Job 27:5–6).

Integrity Affects Behavior

Many have offered helpful insights into integrity:

- Stephen Covey remarks, "Integrity is honestly matching words and feelings with thoughts and actions, with no desire other than for the good of others, without malice or desire to deceive, take advantage, manipulate, or control; constantly reviewing your intent as you strive for congruence."[1]
- Patrick Morley declares, "Integrity is a one-to-one correlation between my Bible, my beliefs, and my behavior."[2]
- Henry Blackaby writes, "Integrity of character occurs when there is consistency between actions and inner convictions over time."[3]

In short, integrity is *a sound wholeness in which your walk matches your talk over time, grounded on the belief system of your life.* As I look around I become more and more convinced that behavior is determined by belief. What we do is determined by who we are.

Clearly, Joseph had settled that issue. Integrity was at the core of the metal of his very being. In this book, we've covered several incidents that showed this facet of Joseph's character. When asked by his father to check on his critical-hearted brothers, his integrity led him to do so, even when his feelings could have pulled in the other direction. Having been placed in charge of Potiphar's holdings, his integrity would not allow him to take what was not his—Potiphar's wife—even when freely offered. Even in prison, Joseph proved himself to be trustworthy. When he eventually was released from prison and rose to a high level of power, he had opportunity to wreak vengeance on the brothers who had mistreated him. But it was Joseph's character that caused him instead to help them.

A Sought-After Commodity

You don't have to look far to find that integrity is in demand. The former chairman of J. C. Penney Company, Don Seibert, has said, "Among the people I know at the top of the nation's major corporations, the personal quality that is regarded most highly is a solid, unwavering sense of integrity. The higher a person moves up in business, the more important it is for his peers and superiors to feel they can depend on his word. They have to know that he's a 'straight shooter' in every sense of the word, one who won't cut moral corners to further his own interests."[4]

Peter Drucker's book, *Management Tasks, Responsibilities and Practices*, supports that ideal with research. Drucker reported that of 1300 senior executives questioned, seventy-one percent listed integrity first among sixteen major traits needed for business success.[5]

But that's not really a surprise. It's true in everyday life, too. Whom do you want to be surrounded by—people with or without integrity?

Do you want to be able to take your spouse's word to the bank? When a colleague says he or she will meet a deadline, do you want to be able to depend on it? When your children say they're going to a certain place when they leave home with friends, do you want to know with certainty that's exactly where they're headed? When you go to the drive-in deposit lane at your bank, does it put you at ease to know you can trust the teller to deposit your money in your account? When the pastor teaches from the Scripture, is it important to you for him to actually live what he preaches? When the surgeon says you need an operation, do you prefer to trust that the medical degree on his wall is legitimate?

All of us realize how important integrity is. The key is not simply that the other guy has it, but that we take responsibility for it in our own lives. A recent commercial portrayed the message, "Image is everything." But that's not even close to the truth. Image is only fluff. The truth is that integrity is everything.

I recently read of an unscrupulous salesman who delivered a bid his company had made to an engineering firm. As he was ushered into the office where he was to present his bid, he met the firm's representative. After a brief conversation, the host received a phone call and politely excused himself just for a moment.

The less-than-honest salesman noticed that his competitor's bid was lying on the desk. Unfortunately, a soft drink hid the total amount. He gazed out of the office to see if anyone was looking. He lifted the can and got the surprise of his life—rather than a cold drink, it was a bottomless can filled with BBs. The quiet office was filled with the resounding sound of BBs racing across a hardwood floor. The firm's representative immediately opened the office door, saw the circumstances, and escorted the salesman to the door. In the business world, and in everyday life, integrity matters.

Grounded in a Belief System

The wholeness of the metal that supports our lives is determined by what we believe. I see the Bible as God's owner's manual for my successful living. Did you know that, according to research, the most unread book in America is the car owner's manual? I've asked hundreds of audiences how many have read theirs. There are always a select few, but by far the overwhelming majority don't.

Yet the car owner's manual is written for us to avoid breakdowns and to maximize the performance of the vehicle we have purchased. Likewise, God gave us His owner's manual, the Bible, to help us avoid breakdowns—morally, ethically, spiritually, and relationally—and to operate at peak performance. His greatest desire is that we develop a wholeness in our lives that allows our walk to match our talk because it is based on a solid belief system.

That belief system is the internal compass that guides our steps. For this reason, Jesus warned that external circumstances don't cause the biggest problem, but rather the inner condition of our hearts. Jesus told the crowd around Him, "Nothing outside a man can make him 'unclean' by going into him. Rather, it is what comes out of a man that makes him 'unclean' . . . Don't you see that nothing that enters a man from the outside can make him 'unclean'? For it doesn't go into his heart but into his stomach, and then out of his body . . . What comes out of a man is what makes him 'unclean.' For from within, out of men's hearts, come evil thoughts, sexual immorality, theft, murder, adultery, greed, malice, deceit, lewdness, envy, slander, arrogance and folly. All these evils come from inside and make a man 'unclean'" (Mark 7:15–23).

Public Impact Is Determined by Private Strength

We carry our real, true belief system in our hearts. That's exactly why the psalmist said, "I have hidden your word in my heart / that I might not sin against you" (Ps. 119:11). When people ask me what advice I would give above everything else, here's what I say: *Set a guard on your heart.*

But how can a person do that? Let me give you a few suggestions:

1. Make a personal commitment. Joseph obviously had made a commitment that he would not allow his heart to be polluted by ungodly attitudes or actions. He had drawn a line in the sand over which he would not step. I have found it wise to draw that line early, in preparation for temptation. And once that line is drawn, it's a good idea to step backward and draw a second line, a little more strictly, and never cross that line either. The decision of the will can make all the difference. F. W. Borham hit the nail on the head when he said, "We make our decisions, and then our decisions turn around and make us."[6] It is repeatedly evidenced in Joseph's character that he had, indeed, drawn his lines.

2. Beware of compromise. Like Joseph, we need to purpose in our hearts that we won't go against God's standards. Yet everywhere we turn, forces pull us to make an exception. It's no different than our ancestors Adam and Eve. Satan's first line of attack was, "Did God really say . . . ?" The strategy has never changed. The temptation to compromise always comes in the same form. And if we're not careful, we'll rationalize with answers such as . . .

- "This one time won't make a difference."
- "Nobody will ever know."
- "I won't have the same weakness that others have had."

- "I can only do it once, and then I'll stop."
- "What's the big deal about one little try?"

You know exactly what I mean. You may have even heard better lines than these in your mind and heart. What you do at that point speaks volumes about what you really believe about God and His Word.

3. Guard your character. Character doesn't just affect your behavior when other people are watching. It affects your behavior—period. Joseph's ability to withstand temptation was an outward expression of his inner strength. It was the stamp on his life that marked him as belonging to God. It was his recognition that ultimately sin would be an affront to the One who was most important in his life. That's why, when his boss's wife attempted to seduce him, Joseph replied, "No one is greater in this house than I am. My master has withheld nothing from me except you, because you are his wife. *How then could I do such a wicked thing and sin against God?*" (Gen. 39:9, italics added). Joseph's character enabled him to make that stand, because he was the same person in public as he was in private—a person who sought to reflect God's character to the world.

4. Focus your concentration. Recognize that the battle will be won or lost in your mind. A long-standing computer maxim is "garbage in, garbage out." It doesn't just apply to computers—it applies to you. That's why the apostle Paul wrote, "Whatever is true, whatever is noble, whatever is right, whatever is pure, whatever is lovely, whatever is admirable—if anything is excellent or praiseworthy—think about such things" (Phil. 4:8).

In our visually-oriented society, it's also important to remember that your eyes are one of the primary conduits through which your mind receives information. Just before Eve succumbed to the serpent's temptation, Scripture says she noticed that the fruit on the forbidden tree was "pleasing to the eye" (Gen. 3:6). Your life will follow the direction where your eyes are focused. Even with that in mind, it's important to admit that you may not be totally able to control the things that flash before your eyes and onto the screen of your mind. But you can control what *stays* there!

5. Keep your insides clean. God's book teaches us to keep short accounts with Him. When we make a mistake, He invites us to quickly acknowledge it. That's what confession is all about—agreeing with God that what has happened is sin and it is an offense to His holy character. It is a realization that we have broken God's heart by our actions. It is an admission that what we have said, done, thought, or neglected contradicts His Word. It's a statement that we need to change.

Scripture says that if we are faithful and regularly admit, confess, and take responsibility for our sin, God is even more faithful to forgive it and to wipe it clean from our lives. You'll find that clearly expressed in 1 John 1:9. But read the rest of the book and you'll find that the act of saying "I'm sorry" *without changing the behavior* is inconsistent with God's Word. John's epistle makes it very clear that if somebody is really committed to following Him, knowing Him, and obeying Him, that person cannot simply shrug at sin and say, "I'm sorry," only to go back to it in the near future. God expects that, when we have confessed, we won't make a beeline to return to the sin. A key part of that confession is repentance. Repentance does not simply mean to feel remorse. It means to change direction 180 degrees. It is to leave behind any attitude or action that doesn't meet the standard expressed in God's Word.

6. *Remember, everything counts.* In the first chapter we talked about how people tend to establish a sort of "sin continuum"—a scale that somehow ranks sins from the "smallies" to the "biggies." But in the real world, that continuum just doesn't work. Even in the secular world, we eventually find that everything counts. The "smallies" are just as crucial as the biggies.

Several years ago, I heard of a financial company whose chief executive officer was retiring. The directors met and determined to promote someone from within the company. They interviewed three vice presidents and then voted in a closed meeting to determine which candidate would become the new CEO. They selected a dynamic young man and agreed to bring him in after lunch and make the announcement. With the major decision accomplished, the board recessed for lunch.

One board member went to the company's snack bar to enjoy a few quiet moments along with a quick bite. The newly chosen leader happened to be in line just ahead of him, but the young man didn't notice him. As they moved toward the register, the director saw the young man take some pats of butter and hide them under his napkin.

Returning to the directors' meeting, the board member shared the unfortunate incident. Lively discussion ensued. Finally the young man was summoned. "We were going to announce that you had been chosen as the new leader of this company," the chairman told him. "Unfortunately, the scenario has changed. At lunch, you took some butter without paying for it. Instead of promoting you, this board is asking for your immediate resignation."

If the secular world recognizes the need for that type of integrity, we who call ourselves Christians surely must require it of ourselves.

Metal That Will Last

When there is integrity in the metal, it will last and serve well, whatever its use. I've noticed that when integrity is strongly present, a few qualities will inevitably flow in its wake:

1. Humility. Senator Mark Hatfield has said that humility is one of the most important aspects of character and integrity. And, he adds, one of the greatest tests of humility is criticism. Zeroing in on the issue, Hatfield said, "The real test of humility is how you handle criticism . . . the humble way to handle criticism is to try to understand the reasons for the criticism, to look for what worth there might be in it."[7]

The apostle Peter exhorted Christians to "humble yourselves, therefore, under God's mighty hand, that he may lift you up in due time" (1 Pet. 5:6). Notice a key issue . . . God wants us to humble ourselves. He doesn't want to have to do it for us. When we neglect this task so that He has to take over, the humbling process is far less than comfortable. But I've noticed repeatedly those with a deep foundation of integrity tend to have girders of steel in the area of humility.

2. Authority. William Oncken, who taught at the California Institute of Technology, called integrity "the authority of character" and said it may well be the most important type of authority achieved over a lifetime. In his words, your integrity is your "credit rating" with other people. "Obviously," he says, "you will get more and better action from a man who has respect for your character than from one who hasn't." And the gauge other people use to measure your character is based on "how far you have been willing to put yourself out to maintain your record of honesty and dependability . . . The greater their respect, the farther they'll go, and the greater is the component of character in your overall authority."[8]

Joseph's Character Earns Authority

You can see this principle demonstrated in Joseph's life. While Pharaoh's cupbearer served time in prison, he had a disturbing dream. Joseph was able to interpret it for him and tell him what it meant for his future. When the cupbearer left prison, he promptly forgot about Joseph . . . until the Pharaoh had a couple of disturbing dreams, and no one could tell him what they meant.

The cupbearer told his king about the man in prison who had successfully interpreted *his* dream. Joseph, who had now spent two years in prison for a crime he didn't commit, was summarily released from his cell and taken to the king. He listened to Pharaoh describe nightmares, and then he explained that God was using these dreams to warn Pharaoh about a coming famine. The now thirty-year-old Joseph quickly outlined a plan that would save the nation of Egypt.

Pharaoh responded, "Can we find anyone like this man [Joseph], one in whom is the spirit of God?" (Gen. 41:38). Then he gave Joseph overwhelming authority when he said, "Since God has made all this known to you . . . you shall be in charge of my palace, and all my people are to submit to your orders. Only with respect to the throne will I be greater than you" (Gen. 41:39–40).

You see, Joseph was not just a good student of integrity—he was a good practitioner. People of every rank in life came to respect him, because they knew they could trust him. Time and time again, he rose to a position of authority—in Potiphar's house, in the prison, and then finally in the whole land of Egypt. People knew they could trust him. The metal of his life was indelibly stamped with integrity as he imitated the character of his God.

But how about you—what's stamped on your life?

Putting Yourself in the Refiner's Hands

1. In your own words, define *integrity* and *character*.
2. Describe how you know if another person has integrity.
3. How does your belief system impact your behavior?
4. List the six steps involved in guarding your heart.
5. On a grading scale like you saw in school—A through F—give yourself a grade for each of the six steps listed above.

   What areas of your life don't yet bear the indelible stamp of God's character?

TEN

Removing the Impurities of Unforgiveness and Bitterness

I GREW UP IN THE MIDWEST. STEEL PLANTS formed a significant part of that region's city skylines. Gary, Indiana. Chicago, Illinois. Detroit, Michigan. Pittsburgh, Pennsylvania. Those smokestacks were so common that movies shot in Midwest locations inevitably featured their presence.

Each steel mill had, at its center, at least one blast furnace, towering some ninety feet in height. Iron ore—red hot from the burning of its fuel called *coke*—would be introduced into the furnace. As it combined with the inner environment of limestone, the hiss of carbon monoxide signaled the ore's melting. Sparks flew. Steam draped the furnace like summer storm clouds clinging to a mountain. Workers wearing shielded helmets, their clothes soaked with sweat, constantly watched valves to make sure the pressure stayed within its crucial range.

The iron ore, combined with charcoal in the furnace, was heated to the molten state by a forced draft of air. As the solid iron dissolved into liquid, a slag or dross, composed of metallic impurities and charcoal ash, formed at the top. Every two hours the slag would be drawn off so as not to contaminate the iron itself. Were it not to be drawn off, the metal would be full of impurities and therefore dangerously inadequate for commercial use. The more demanding the final use of the steel, the more critical it was that the impurities be removed, lest the product be ruined.

So it is with our lives. The slag of unforgiveness and bitterness can literally ruin the mettle of our lives. Its presence inevitably weakens our character and contribution. Over some twenty-five years in ministry, I have found that about seventy percent of the problems for which I have counseled people inevitably go back to a core impurity of unforgiveness and bitterness.

Joseph's life demonstrates how a forgiving heart strengthens the steel of our lives. It restores ruptured relationships. It heals wounded feelings. It removes the slag of resentment. It makes us productive and useable.

Keeping Accounts Clear

When I was in high school, I worked in a women's shoe store. My introduction to the business world was both stimulating and educational. I didn't just learn about sales—I learned about life. Each evening, after the store closed, we opened the cash register and pulled the long tape that recorded the day's sales. We checked the tape carefully, marked it, and then filed it away. Then we cleared the cash register so we could begin with a new accounting of sales the following morning.

Joseph demonstrated that forgiveness is a lot like that daily accounting. He somehow was able to clear all the accounts and start over with the people who had hurt him. Of all of the marvelous things that Joseph achieved, I am most amazed by his attitude of forgiveness. He somehow managed to get beyond the need for revenge—even with his brothers who had attacked him and sold him into slavery. He literally forgot their hostility and abuse. He was able to act and respond as if those injuries had never occurred. Joseph's miraculous ability to forgive is revealed in the names he gave to his sons.

What's in a Name?

After he became Egypt's prime minister, Joseph married a young woman named Asenath, and they had two sons. In biblical culture, names meant a great deal. They said something significant about the character of the individual or about his circumstances. So the names that Joseph gave his sons are notable.

- *Manasseh* means "to forget." Joseph gave his reasoning for the name when he said, "It is because God has made me forget all my trouble and all my father's household" (Gen. 41:51).
- *Ephraim* means "twice fruitful." Again, Joseph explained, "It is because God has made me fruitful in the land of my suffering" (41:52).

Joseph could never have forgotten all of the family mess if he had not first forgiven. Forgetting and forgiving go together—like a lock and key. And forgiving must always come first. It won't work if you get them turned around.

So what can we learn from Joseph's example?

False Forgiveness

Many of us labor under some false assumptions about forgiveness. Those conjectures encourage us to rationalize our action or inaction instead of pursuing genuine forgiveness. Let's take a moment to correct those mistaken ideas:

1. Forgiveness is not mere tolerance. It's easy to excuse ourselves from actually forgiving if we decide instead to simply tolerate the person who has offended us. We wear a hypocritical mask and sigh our acceptance of this cruel martyrdom. We coldly acknowledge the person, even wincing a smile in his presence. Any remaining friendship is skin-deep at best—and sometimes that skin crawls when we're with the offender.

The worst part is that we justify our actions, even congratulating ourselves because we have not totally turned away from the person who hurt us. We convince ourselves that whatever happened is entirely the other person's fault. And we commend ourselves for not exacting revenge. We convince ourselves that just putting up with this "snake in the grass" is going the "second mile."

No meaningful resolution can occur under such conditions. The best we can hope for is a stalemate, and, generally, the relationship will continue to degenerate as wounded feelings fester.

2. Forgiveness is not ignoring the problem. Some people think they achieve forgiveness by pretending nothing happened. To acknowledge the conflict would somehow be a sign of weakness. Rather than admitting weakness, they develop a defense mechanism. But problems never disappear simply because we ignore them. Usually they grow as resentment escalates.

3. Forgiveness is not found in empty words. Words are cheap. To merely say, "I'm sorry" or "you're forgiven" is easy. But forgiveness goes beyond words—it's a matter of the will. Certainly, words express forgiveness. But without the support of the will, the words are nothing more than a hollow, meaningless exchange of verbiage. The will undergirds a moral commitment to intentionally bring the hurt to an end.

True Forgiveness

False forgivenness is counterproductive. It nurses the wound, sometimes blowing the initial hurt out of proportion and magnifying the original problem. It encourages resentment and pride and builds a desire for revenge.

True forgiveness, on the other hand, absorbs the hurt and erases it. Webster's dictionary defines forgiveness like this: "To give up resentment against or the desire to punish; to stop being angry with; to pardon."

Forgiveness demands that I let go of resentment. It requires me to release my bitterness, hurt, and pride. I must decide that the relationship is more valuable than my need to be right. Since there are two sides to every conflict, I may even have to admit that I had something to do with the original rift in the relationship. David Augsburger, in his excellent book *Caring Enough to Forgive*, states, "Significant movement toward forgetting begins as we bring an end to blaming and move toward the recognition of our joint participation, to whatever degree, in the painful situation."[1]

Joseph somehow knew the value of this kind of true forgiveness—this willingness to face his hurts and intentionally put them aside, not holding them against the perpetrators. And interestingly enough, he may have learned this from his family. Joseph's own father had a unique opportunity to experience forgiveness, and Joseph was there to see it.

Jacob, Joseph's father, also known as Israel, had tricked his twin brother Esau out of a portion of his rightful inheritance. Jacob fled his brother's wrath, but many years later he had to return home. He loaded up his large family and all of his possessions and started on the long journey. Dreading the possibilities, Scripture says he was "in great fear and distress" (Gen. 32:7).

When Esau came to meet him, he brought four hundred men. It's bad enough to have to face one you have wronged . . . but when he brings an army—what could be worse? Jacob naturally thought they had come to attack. Instead, amazingly, Esau forgave. The Bible records that "Esau ran to meet Jacob and embraced him; he threw his arms around his neck and kissed him. And they wept" (Gen. 33:4). Jacob responded, "To see your face is like seeing the face of God, now that you have received me favorably" (Gen. 33:10).

Jacob captured his own relief as he expressed this great truth. Forgiveness is the clearest—and perhaps the most exacting—imitation of God's character. Joseph had seen that expressed in his father's life, and he willingly followed his uncle's example as he extended forgiveness to those who had hurt him. But, in doing so, he was also following God's example.

God Sets the Example

God never expects us to do anything He has not already done Himself. In this difficult area of forgiveness, His example is the clearest and most relevant. He has forgiven you and me.

You see, our sin is an affront to God. It offends Him. And until we accept His offer of forgiveness, our relationship with Him is one of alienation. No one knew that better than David. Following his sinful relationship with Bathsheba, David found that God is always ready and willing to grant forgiveness. Scholars believe it took as long as a year for David to experience renewal in his relationship with God, but when that happened, he recorded the contrast in his feelings. He wrote, "Blessed is he / whose transgressions are forgiven, / whose sins are covered. / Blessed is the man / whose sin the LORD does not count against him / and in whose spirit is no deceit. / When I kept silent, / my bones wasted away / through my groaning all day long. / For day and night / your hand was heavy upon me; / my strength was sapped / as in the heat of summer" (Ps. 32:1–4).

David's feelings are our feelings. Ruptured relationships are miserable relationships. And when we rupture our relationship with God by our sin, life comes apart at the seams. When we choose not to pursue reconciliation, we pay a heavy price. Guilt weighs like a heavy hand, pressing hard upon heart and mind. And because we waste so much emotional energy in dealing with the guilt, we lose the stamina and physical energy for effective daily living.

God continually stands ready to remedy that situation. He is more ready to forgive than we are to receive that forgiveness. And when He forgives, He forgives completely. The Bible says, "As far as the east is from the west, / so far has he removed our transgressions from us" (Ps. 103:12). The New Testament carries on with the same theme, proclaiming our forgiveness through Jesus Christ. Because He was willing to bear the death that should have been ours—the penalty that should have been the direct consequence of our sin—we have the opportunity to restore our relationship with God if we sincerely ask for and accept His forgiveness. The key to continually maintaining that intimate fellowship is in seeking forgiveness on a regular basis.

By His actions, God painted a portrait of the true nature and expression of forgiveness. Knowing that we humans are totally incapable of doing anything to earn our way back into His favor, He takes the initiative. He seeks us out and extends His hand. His offer is motivated by nothing but love, for true forgiveness does not grow from the expectation that someone will do something for you. God's example requires that we take the initiative and grant forgiveness, but we must do it without a hidden agenda.

God Leaves No Other Option

Beyond giving an example, God clearly stated His expectations for our behavior in a series of directives that are worded as commands. God did not allow for a Plan B when it comes to forgiveness. Here are just a few of His demands:

- "Be kind and compassionate to one another, forgiving each other, just as in Christ God forgave you." (Eph. 4:32)
- "Bear with each other and forgive whatever grievances you may have against one another. Forgive as the Lord forgave you." (Col. 3:13)
- "For if you forgive men when they sin against you, your heavenly Father will also forgive you. But if you do not forgive men their sins, your Father will not forgive your sins." (Matt. 6:14–15)

God leaves little doubt as to what he expects in our relationships. He says nothing about who is right and who is wrong. He simply calls us to practice forgiveness.

That kind of action can only be motivated by godly love—not a weak, sentimental feeling, but a willful determination. Love based on mere emotion has no staying power. Real love, which is rooted in one's will, "guts it out" when things get difficult. In one of the most poetic passages in all of Scripture, the apostle Paul described it like this: "Love is patient, love is kind. It does not envy, it does not boast, it is not proud. It is not rude, it is not self-seeking, it is not easily angered, it keeps no record of wrongs. Love does not delight in evil but rejoices with the truth. It always protects, always trusts, always hopes, always perseveres. Love never fails" (1 Cor. 13:4–8).

He could have easily substituted the word *forgiveness* for each reference to love, for the two go hand in hand. But you and I can only experience that kind of loving forgiveness as God changes our hearts.

Filling in the Details

When it comes to forgiveness, God doesn't leave the details to us. He gives the command, but He also explains how we are to accomplish this difficult feat. He doesn't leave it in the theoretical but puts it into concrete practicality. And that practicality hits us right smack in the middle of our daily living.

There are basically two situations in which forgiveness must be exercised: when we are offended, and when we offend someone else. God speaks poignantly to both circumstances.

1. When we are offended. Jesus' disciple Peter was always trying to be in the spotlight. He wanted to look good. He always wanted to have the right answer. Once, when he was feeling especially spiritual, he asked Jesus how often we are to forgive others. He hinted that forgiving somebody as many as seven times would put us in the super-good category. His statement was based on rabbinical law, which required that a person be forgiven three times.

Without hesitating, Jesus gave an answer which popped Peter's spiritual bubble. "I tell you, not seven times, but seventy-seven times" (Matt. 18:22). Some manuscripts actually say "seventy times seven."

Then He told a story about a king who was going through his books one day and discovered an entry for one of his servants who owed him a large sum of money—perhaps the equivalent of ten million dollars. The man was unable to pay the debt, so the king basically decided to sell this man's possessions, and also to sell the man and his wife and children into slavery to collect the money. But the servant begged the king to be patient and give him a chance to repay the amount on his own. The king actually forgave the debt in full—an important point considering the rest of the story.

Then that servant found another man who owed him a relatively small debt. He demanded payment, and when the man was unable to comply, he had the poor soul thrown into debtors' prison.

When the king heard about this, he was terribly angry. This servant had not followed his example of forgiveness. He confronted the man saying, "Shouldn't you have had mercy on your fellow servant just as I had on you?" (Matt. 18:33). The story concludes by noting, "In anger his master turned him over to the jailers to be tortured, until he should pay back all he owed" (Matt. 18:34).

Then Jesus drove home the point. He told Peter and the others who were there, "This is how my heavenly Father will treat each of you unless you forgive your brother from your heart" (Matt. 18:35).

Christ used this story to illustrate the boundlessness of God's mercy. Regardless of how drastic the breach of relationship, God stands ready to restore it. But He noted that God expects us to show the same attitude toward those who wrong us. If we fail to do so, the result will be disastrous. Anger and bitterness will incarcerate us in a self-induced torture chamber.

As we sit in our self-made prison and lick our festering wounds, we will soon find that unforgiveness exacts a huge price in every part of our being. An inability to forgive gives birth to an inability to accept forgiveness. That impacts us spiritually and emotionally. Doctors note that anger and resentment also yield physical results in the form of high blood pressure, migraine headaches, spastic colons, and other maladies that could be avoided if we simply were willing to release people from the emotional debt we believe they owe us.

In this life, we cannot entirely avoid hurtful situations. That's part of what happens in a world that is marred by sin. It's not a question of *if* they will happen—it's *when* they will happen. So how do you handle situations where you have been hurt? Do you cling tenaciously to your resentment? Let me challenge you to take the following important steps instead:

- Remember God's willingness to forgive you.
- Recall that He expects you to do the same for others.
- Realize that you must take the first step toward resolving the conflict.
- Recognize that it's a matter of your will and not your emotions.

- Remember that you are not responsible for the other person's reaction—only for taking the initiative.
- Recognize that refusal to offer forgiveness places you in the category of a hypocrite.

Jean Paul Richter, a German writer of an earlier century, compares this kind of forgiveness to the making of a pearl. When you choose to forgive, he said, the individual who has pierced your heart becomes like a seaworm that stabs through the shell of an oyster. But what is the result of that wound? The oyster "straightway closes the wound with a pearl."[2]

I like that analogy, and I believe that as you embrace the lifestyle of forgiveness, you will find you are creating for yourself a string of pearls—a wealth of treasure that exceeds your comprehension.

2. When we offend someone else. From my counseling experience, I've learned that often it's not enough to deal with reality. Perceived reality sometimes is the root of the problem rather than actual fact. What does that mean to this discussion? Well, it means that sometimes we offend people inadvertently. God doesn't give us the luxury of ignoring the situation or of justifying ourselves because we didn't mean it. We must be willing to deal with that individual's perception of what happened.

Christ clearly explained this when He said, "If you are offering your gift at the altar and there remember that your brother has something against you, leave your gift there in front of the altar. First go and be reconciled to your brother; then come and offer your gift" (Matt. 5:23–24).

Notice, Jesus made no mention of who is at fault. He simply said that for some reason your brother has something against you. It may even be something he has perceived rather than something that is real. But as far as Jesus is concerned, the crucial point is the breach in the relationship.

God puts the burden on the shoulders of the one who has somehow offended the other person. He doesn't say to wait until your brother gets a better perception of reality. Nor does He allow you just to pray about it, hoping it will resolve itself. He says instead, go to your brother and try to make things right. This must happen even before we worship.

Perhaps you have recently felt a certain distance from God. You just don't seem to be getting through to the Father when you pray. Could it be the result of an unresolved conflict? Have you intentionally or unintentionally hurt someone?

I remember a strain that developed between another person and me. I was angry at him, and I walked away from the friendship. Months dragged by, and my fury began to take its toll as hurtful thoughts consumed my time and zapped my energy. While I was sitting around waiting for him to take the first step toward reconciliation, I read those verses in Matthew. I realized it was my responsibility to attempt to bridge the gap.

During the months of our "cold war" I had lost track of him. I finally found that he had moved to another state. Picking up the phone, I dialed his number. When I heard his voice, I almost hung up. But I knew I couldn't. I told him why I had called and asked if he would forgive me for allowing the rupture to occur in our relationship. Immediately I felt that my spirit had been released from bondage. But I also learned that the initial act of giving and receiving forgiveness is just the first step . . . but a critical and valuable first step.

The Value of Forgiveness

Do you realize the value placed on the ability to blot out mistakes? Of course, in our economy of emotions, the value placed on forgiveness may very well depend on the size of the original offense. But sometimes the act of wiping the slate clean for an individual will actually save that person's life.

Harry Ironside used to tell a story about a young man who served in the Russian army during the time of Czar Nicholas I. Because his father was a friend to the czar, this young man had been entrusted with great responsibility. He handled the payroll in one of the barracks. Unfortunately, the young man's character didn't measure up to the responsibility. It seems he had an affection for gambling, and eventually he took to "borrowing" from the payroll money, intending to pay it back, of course, but never winning enough to stay ahead of his debts.

One day the man received notice that the czar's representative was coming to check his accounts. That evening he got out the books to see the exact state of the funds that had been entrusted to him. Seeing the vast difference between the amount he owed and the amount he owned, he knew he was about to experience the worst disgrace of his life. He resolved to take his own life.

This young man pulled out his revolver and placed it on the table in front of him. He briefly wrote an explanation of the situation, and at the bottom of the ledger he wrote, "A great debt! Who can pay?"

He decided that, at the stroke of midnight, he would pull the trigger and kill himself. And he sat, watching the clock, and waiting.

But in the meantime, the young man became drowsy and dozed off. Jerking himself awake in the middle of the night, he turned his bleary eyes to the clock and realized it was long after his appointed time of death. He reached for his revolver . . . but as he did so, his eyes crossed over the ledger and he read his own message. "A great debt! Who can pay?"

Underneath those words, there was one single signature—"Nicholas."

Apparently the czar, walking in the evening, had seen the light in the barracks and had entered. Seeing the young man's plight, and reading the ledger sheet, he quickly understood what had happened. In a surge of magnanimity, the czar had willingly signed his own offer to pay the debt. And according to Ironside, the young man rested on that promise. The next morning a messenger arrived from the palace. He carried exactly the amount of money needed to cover the deficit. Because of his willingness to forgive the young man, and to forget his irresponsible actions, the czar did much more than just pay off a debt—he saved a life.[3]

Forgiving and Forgetting

Many of us will never face the necessity of offering to forgive such a huge financial debt as did Czar Nicholas. But all of us will, at one time or another, have to forgive other people for offending or hurting us. In those times, Joseph stands for all time as a prime example of forgiveness. But he went to a higher level—he intentionally put those offenses behind him and literally forgot them. As we noted at the beginning of this chapter, the name of his son Manasseh is clear evidence of this decision.

But what exactly does that mean? Did he lose his ability to recall the hurtful events if his life? Did he forget the pit? The prison? The false accusations? The darkened cell?

Of course not.

Joseph remembered the events, but he chose to forget the pain. Rather than allowing bitterness to spoil his present and future, he put aside the past. He understood that he could do nothing to change his history, but he did have control over his present and his future—and how he handled those two precious commodities would make all the difference in the world.

When the Confederate army was finally defeated in the Civil War, Abraham Lincoln was asked how he was going to treat the rebellious Southerners. The question seemed to open a wide door for him to express his frustration and disgust with the entire conflict. It would be his opportunity to mandate severe punishment for those who had rebelled. Unexpectedly, however, the merciful president simply said, "I will treat them as if they had never been away." That was all he would ever say. He would never pull to the forefront even his expectation for people to remember his incredible act of forgiveness. Isn't it interesting that most of us, even when we do forgive and attempt to forget, just don't want other people to forget what we forgave!

Paul was dealing with this same struggle when he wrote, "One thing I do: Forgetting what is behind and straining toward what is ahead, I press on toward the goal to win the prize for which God has called me heavenward in Christ Jesus" (Phil. 3:13–14).

Paul intentionally put away the memory of his successes, but he also refused to recall the false accusations, beatings, disappointments, and criticisms. He had learned that forgiving is the first step—forgetting is the follow-through. Both require that we separate the offending person from his or her action. Then we find the ability and opportunity to love the person while not necessarily loving the act.

On April 24, 1985, I clipped an Ann Landers column from the *Charlotte Observer*. The column contained a letter from a woman who had been married some thirty years and assumed she had a faithful husband. She had been shocked to discover he was having an affair. Sleepless nights and buckets of tears later, she asked Ann Landers if she should forgive and forget. Ann Landers' response could have been put side by side with the scriptural advice we have read.

> "Dear D: You must forgive and forget—for YOUR sake, not his. Let the past bury its dead and look ahead to a new and better life. It is there if you want it. I realize this is easier said than done. You will need a lot of counseling to get the rage out. But it will be well worth the time and trouble. The alternative is ultimate self-destruction."

Don't Choose Self-destruction

Ann Landers used some strong words to describe the person who refuses to forgive. She said the only alternative is self-destruction.

I pray you don't choose that road. Choose instead to revive broken relationships by offering the free gift of forgiveness. As David Augsburger explains, "True forgiveness restores the other's freedom with no questions asked, no demands imposed, no repentance required, no revenge attempted . . . it sees true repentance *as an emotion rising from the experience of forgiveness.* When one knows that he has been loved, accepted, forgiven, then he is free to respond repentantly" (italics added).[4] The act of forgiving and forgetting brings healing for damaged emotions and feelings. It renews the circulation of love, acceptance, and hope, which are as crucial to the health of our relationships as blood is to our bodies.

The story of Jamie Koehler illustrates this concept. Jamie, fifteen, was on his way home from a day of swimming with his friends in Michigan. Suddenly the car in which he was riding slammed into a car turning in front of them. Not wearing a seat belt, Jamie was thrown through the windshield. In the impact, his nose was sheared from his face.

Miraculously, some quick thinking emergency personnel and a very gifted doctor at the hospital, Dr. Dennis Hammond, performed the unthinkable.

Emergency personnel at the scene of the accident found Jamie's nose, wrapped it in gauze, and packed it in ice. Arriving at the hospital, Dr. Hammond, who had just received training in microsurgery, quickly evaluated the situation. In an operation that would last nine hours, Hammond used watchmaker-sized instruments and microscopes to reattach the nose. Two tiny arteries and one vein were reconstructed and sutured to allow blood to once again flow to the appendage. The arteries and veins were between .4 to .3 millimeters in diameter—about the size of a sharpened pencil lead. The sutures used to replace the veins and arteries were finer than human hair. With the blood flow restored, Koehler's nose was saved.[5]

Microsurgery has been used to reattach arms, hands, fingers, toes, and ears. One of the key essentials is replacing the blood flow to the severed body parts. It is the blood that brings the life back to the injured area.

Likewise, forgiveness restores the circulation of love, acceptance, and hope. Damaged emotions can function again. Ruptured feelings can be restored. Bruised and damaged egos can be healed. Relationships can once again flourish.

Forgiveness Is a "Hinge"

Jesus made it clear that forgiveness is not an option. In fact, He included this fact in the prayer that He taught to His disciples—the Lord's Prayer. I heard of one little boy who mistakenly recited it like this: "And forgive us our trash passes as we forgive those who pass trash against us." Most of us can do a better job of quoting the actual words, but we don't get to the point of really understanding what Jesus meant. He implied that forgiveness is like a hinge—one side is our ability to forgive, and the other side is our ability to receive forgiveness. Neither side of the hinge will work on its own.

So if you need to forgive someone, or if you need to receive forgiveness from someone, I challenge you to pursue it today. Whether you have been the one offended or the one perceived as the offender, you must take the initiative. Do whatever is required to remove the slag, the dross, from your life. Don't let the impurities ruin the mettle of your character and contribution. Write that person or call or make a visit. I promise you—you'll sense a new freedom in your relationship with the Lord, and a new zest in your life.[6]

Putting Yourself in the Refiner's Hands

1. Briefly describe how you came to accept God's forgiveness and how it has changed your life.

2. How has your relationship with God changed your understanding of forgiveness?
3. In your own words, describe the process that Scripture requires:
   a. If you have been offended or hurt by someone.
   b. If you have intentionally or unintentionally offended or hurt someone.
4. If we are unable to forgive those who have wronged us, how does that affect our relationship with God?
5. List anyone you need to forgive, or anyone from whom you need to seek forgiveness.

   How and when will you take care of the broken relationships you listed?

ELEVEN

When Tender Love Requires the Strength of Steel

IN HIS SERMON ON THE MOUNT, JESUS TOLD us, "Blessed are the peacemakers, for they will be called sons of God" (Matt. 5:9).

It's a good thing that God promises to bless them, because frankly, peacemakers have a thankless job. Just think about it—a peace*maker* goes into a situation that is fraught with tension, and he literally and effectively *makes peace* at all costs. Usually a true peacemaker bears deep scars, because he absorbs wounds rather than responding to them. He disarms emotional explosives and trips emotional land mines. He confronts people with the truth, and then he sticks around to help deal with the fallout.

The peacemaker understands that love is the greatest force in the entire world. But he understands that, while love is often expressed in tenderness, sometimes it must have the strength of steel. Steel's historic value is found in its durability. It withstands overwhelming pressures. It handles radical temperature changes. It guarantees stability. Producing a metal that has these characteristics is precisely the whole point of the refining process.

Refining makes steel strong. The toughness of the steel has a great deal to do with the carbon content and the removal of impurities such as silicone, phosphorus, manganese, and sulfur. As limestone is introduced into the open hearth process, it combines with the impurities to form slag which can be removed. With the heat kept steadily between 2800° and 3000° F for hours, the molten metal reaches the desired carbon content. The molten metal is often tested by withdrawing a small amount from the furnace, cooling it, and examining its physical and chemical properties. When the carbon content has reached the desired level, the furnace is tapped through a hole in the rear and the molten steel flows into a huge ladle. The ladle then pours the steel into molds, assuring the final product has the appropriate and required degree of toughness.

So it is with the product of love in relationships. As love is forged to take on biblical qualities of consistency, it is essential that love have a certain toughness to it. It will be required to face the challenges that will inevitably bring stress and strain to test the very quality of the love relationship.

A True "Man of Steel"

Given that understanding, I think it's safe to say that James Wideman is a true "man of steel." He can speak from experience regarding the value of a love that refuses to ignore difficult situations—the kind of love that gives strength to confront and restore people. Serving now as a missionary with the North American Mission Board of the Southern Baptist Convention, he builds on the experience of stepping tentatively into an emotional battlefield and working through hidden dangers to bring closure to a desperate predicament.

James served as pastor of a church that had endured a series of painful failures from those in leadership. The pastor who preceded him was caught in an immoral act and literally left town within forty-eight hours of being found out. Other staff members had been "less than honest with budget money, continuing to spend it when they were forbidden to do so" and manipulating committees to gain approval for their own agendas.

James arrived on the scene after the church had been without a pastor for thirteen months. He summed up the experience like this: "I knew I was going to have to deal with fall-out from that experience," he said, "but I had no idea how much mistrust had developed" in this congregation.

James felt he was called to a special ministry of "tearing down and rooting up." He and his family paid a tremendous personal price. But today he thankfully reports that the church has moved into a new position of effective ministry. The results are a functioning deacon ministry, two worship services, a growing emphasis on friendship evangelism, the rise of several new and younger leaders, the renovation of the church building, the establishment of a functioning clothing ministry, a prayer ministry, an outreach to a halfway house for women with substance abuse problems, and a youth-led AIDS ministry.

James's experience mirrors Joseph's. Neither sought confrontation, but they didn't back away from it either. Both demonstrated that confrontation is rarely easy. But sometimes it's absolutely necessary—and when handled correctly, it is ultimately a true expression of love.

A Private Glance

I never fully appreciated how difficult it is to balance love with confrontation until God blessed me with three children—all with quite different personalities. Christy, the oldest, gave me my first real lessons in the concept of "tough love."

From the moment Christy was old enough to put her hands around a ball, she exhibited outstanding athletic prowess. Excellent eye-hand coordination. The ability to catch and throw. Quickness. And that innate ability to simply be in the right place at the right time. She quickly mastered every sport she tried. And in the process, she grew to love soccer.

With each passing year, Cheryl and I found it increasingly difficult to maintain that perfect balance between giving our child plenty of opportunities, yet carefully and protectively watching activities and relationships. Sports can be of great value in teaching things like teamwork, cooperation, initiative, healthy competitiveness, and a winning attitude. Unfortunately, like many other activities, sports can also be a seedbed for getting acquainted with the wrong crowd and getting involved in questionable attitudes and actions.

As a teenager, Christy quickly scaled the ladder of success in soccer. Her high school team was second in the state of Florida during her sophomore year, and she reveled in being a starting star. Recruited by numerous traveling teams, she became an accomplished starter on one that was nationally ranked, and her schedule swept our lives into a whirlwind of practices and *travel*, games and *travel*, tournaments and *travel*.

Despite our best efforts to protect Christy from the unfavorable aspects of this lifestyle, we began to see her exhibiting some characteristics that started the alarms ringing in our hearts. A growing independent arrogance. Belligerence when corrected. Short curtness in conversation. A resistance to questions of natural interest concerning her activities.

Perhaps the alarms rang all the more loudly for me because I remembered my own teen years. Deciding to chart my own course and do my own thing. Choices that would cause me and my parents repeated heartache. Friendships and associations that were less than helpful and beneficial.

Our concerns heightened when our phone began ringing late at night. When Cheryl or I would answer, whoever was calling would quickly hang up. Now and again, as I looked deep into Christy's eyes, the things I saw there made the alarms chime even louder. In a society that says parents have no "right" to check up on their kids, we were hesitant to go through her room or look through her things. But finally the alarms were too loud, and we felt we couldn't wait any longer. It seemed as though Satan himself was declaring, "Go ahead. Preach your sermons. Lead your church. Travel and speak. Serve as a leader in the denomination. But I'm coming after your daughter. And I'll come after the other two as well!"

Going into Christy's room, we began to go through her drawers, pockets, and bookbags. Some of the things we found broke our hearts, and they told us that, as much as we had tried to do everything correctly, Christy had chosen to make some bad decisions. We finally had to confront her—I don't know that we've ever faced a more difficult and dreaded time. Caught with the evidence, she exploded—but we lovingly stood firm.

The days that followed were difficult, and at times heart-breaking. Privileges were taken away. Strict guidelines were implemented and enforced. Activities were randomly monitored. For six months, Christy spent time with a wonderful Christian teen organization, fighting to get back on track. And we prayed night and day . . . day and night . . . as we doled out our "tough love."

We learned a lot of painful lessons that were oh-so-important.

- When your child can't look you in the eye when you're talking about a serious subject, you'd better be concerned.
- When you ask a tough question, and your children answer with questions of their own, they're often trying to avoid the issue at hand.
- When your child isn't readily positive on your meeting some of his or her friends, there's usually a good reason why.
- Just because kids go to church doesn't mean they're living what you or the church teaches.

Those days of tough love were some of the most difficult through which we have ever walked. But how faithful God is when we do exactly what He says, even when it's not easy. Today, Christy has attended a wonderful Christian college and is regularly involved in various Christian ministries. As this chapter is written, she is traveling the country, rallying young people to begin the twenty-first century committed to making a difference for Christ.

Our own story reminds me of Jim and Carol Cymbala, who serve at the famous Brooklyn Tabernacle Church in

New York City. Their own daughter Chrissy went through a period in her own life, beginning at age sixteen, when she ran a long way from the Lord. Carol and Jim also had to exhibit tough love, and through those arduous days of doing the right thing, God proved Himself to be incredibly faithful. As a result of that experience, Carol wrote one of my favorite songs of all time. Its words tell the entire story:

> In my moments of fear,
> Through every pain, every tear,
> There's a God who's been faithful to me.
> When my strength was all gone,
> When my heart had no song,
> Still in love He's proved faithful to me.
> Every word He's promised is true;
> What I thought was impossible,
> I've seen my God do.
>
> He's been faithful, faithful to me,
> Looking back, His love and mercy I see.
> Though in my heart I have questioned,
> Even failed to believe,
> Yet He's been faithful, faithful to me.
>
> When my heart looked away,
> The many times I could not pray,
> Still my God, He was faithful to me.
> The days I spent so selfishly,
> Reaching out for what pleased me;
> Even then God was faithful to me.
> Every time I come back to Him,
> He is waiting with open arms,
> And I see once again,
>
> He's been faithful, faithful to me,
> Looking back, His love and mercy I see.
> Though in my heart I have questioned,

Even failed to believe,
Yet He's been faithful, faithful to me.[1]

Positive Confrontation

Of course, the need for "tough love" is not limited to parent-child relationships. As life seems repeatedly to bring us face-to-face with issues of confrontation in various relationships, we all have to work through the answer to a simple question: How are we supposed to handle this uncomfortable process?

Several years ago David Augsburger wrote an outstanding book titled *Caring Enough to Confront*. He suggested that confrontation doesn't have to be a win-lose proposition. He offered a new term: "care-fronting." With this approach he encouraged people to deal with the issue at hand, using maximum information in an atmosphere that produces minimum threat and stress. He goes on to say that, in confrontation, we have five options, which are characterized by these statements of intent:

1. *"I'll get him."* This approach is definitely a win-lose. It assumes that the one confronting is always right and the other one is always wrong. There is no middle ground.
2. *"I'll get out."* This approach is taken by someone who can't stand the discomfort of conflict and sees withdrawal as the answer. This position proves that silence is not always golden—sometimes it's yellow.
3. *"I'll give in."* People with easy-going personalities often prefer this approach. They want to be nice and never make waves. They'll sacrifice anything to maintain a comfortable relationship.
4. *"I'll meet you halfway."* This position assumes that each party has half the truth, so the whole truth cannot be known unless

both sides are incorporated into the solution. This is the ultimate exaggeration of compromise. Unfortunately, if each party has only half of the truth, this position may end up with nothing but half-truths.

5. *"I care enough to confront."* This approach builds on the belief that the relationship must be characterized by honesty and integrity. Within this context, conflict is both neutral and natural, and it is a potential springboard for improving the relationship.

I believe this last stance is the position Joseph took with his brothers. He cared enough to confront them, disarming the explosives in their relational landscape, so the end result would be healing. God calls us to respond in the same way.

Joseph Meets His Brothers

When famine came, it touched not only Egypt, but also the region around it. Knowing that Egypt had stockpiled supplies, Jacob sent his sons (minus Benjamin, the youngest) to seek food. As they arrived, they found themselves before the Egyptian governor. They didn't recognize him as their brother Joseph—and why should they? He was dressed like an Egyptian. He spoke like an Egyptian. He walked like an Egyptian. (OK, maybe that's taking it a bit far, but you get the point.) And as far as they knew, Joseph either had died, or he was a slave. Certainly he could not be the second-in-command for the most powerful nation on earth.

But Joseph recognized *them* immediately. Can you imagine what went through his mind? Can you see the emotional powder kegs lined up and waiting for the fuses to be lit? Joseph had the perfect opportunity to seek revenge. His brothers were at his mercy. The day of "putting them in their place" had finally dawned! He could refuse to sell them food.

Or, if he wanted to speed up the process, he could simply order them to be killed.

Instead, he chose to disarm the ticking time-bombs through caring confrontation.

Setting Up Some Tests

Joseph was creative with his confrontation. Given his history with these brothers, he didn't want to reveal his identity immediately. So he launched a fact-finding initiative, asking the brothers some seemingly routine questions. They told him their home was in Canaan, and he accused them of spying to find where Egypt was unprotected. The brothers began to panic. Unnerved, they replied, "Your servants were twelve brothers, the sons of one man, who lives in the land of Canaan. The youngest is now with our father, and one is no more" (Gen. 42:13).

Joseph learned a great deal from that statement. Because of their unnecessary admission that one of the original brothers was no longer alive, Joseph knew his brothers had carried the guilt of their action for years. He also knew that, in his absence, Jacob's love had shifted to young Benjamin. He had lost his favorite son, Joseph, and he was keeping Benjamin at home, making sure it didn't happen again.

Joseph's response was captivating—he threw the whole lot of them into prison for three days. At the end of that time, he ordered all but one of them to return to their father and bring back the youngest brother. Failure would be an admission that they were indeed spies. This would cost them their lives.

During this stage, their guilt surfaced once more. The Scripture reads: "They said to one another, 'Surely we are being punished because of our brother. We saw how distressed he was when he pleaded with us for his life, but we would not listen; that's why this distress has come upon us.' Reuben replied, 'Didn't I tell you not to sin against the boy? But you wouldn't listen! Now we must give an accounting for his blood'" (Gen. 42:21–22). The brothers had no idea that Joseph could understand them. He used an interpreter so they wouldn't know he spoke their language. When he heard this, he turned away weeping.

Joseph kept one brother in prison and ordered the others to return for young Benjamin. Each received a bag of grain. The silver they had used for payment was secretly placed back in their sacks. Stopping en route back to Canaan, the brothers found the silver. They were innocent, but they knew it would look as if they had dealt fraudulently with the Egyptian government. Genesis 42:28 says their hearts sank and they asked, "What is this that God has done to us?"

Bringing God Back into the Picture

Joseph's method of confrontation forced his brothers to see life's spiritual dimension. They were experiencing firsthand what Scripture means when it says, "Be sure that your sin will find you out" (Num. 32:23). Past wrongs are like relentless hounds. We can never escape until we deal with them.

When the brothers returned home, they reported the events to their father. Staunchly, he refused to let Benjamin go. But Reuben, the level-headed second oldest, stepped in and took responsibility. Preparing gifts and taking double the amount of silver, they returned to Egypt with young Benjamin.

When Joseph saw them coming, he told his steward to prepare a great feast. Rather than being thrilled, the brothers were terrified. Was the governor trying to lull them into a false security? Would he then accuse them of robbery and inflict punishment? They quickly confessed to finding the silver in their bags. Joseph knew his style of confrontation was working. God was sensitizing their consciences. Their confession had not been partial, nor had it been delayed. God was working in their lives.

As the brothers were seated for the banquet, they found themselves placed in the exact order of their ages. They must have wondered how Joseph knew so much about them. And Benjamin's food portion was five times greater than anyone else's. In giving the youngest such an overabundance, Joseph invited any hidden jealousy to show itself. Was their old self-centeredness still in control? Would they resent Benjamin because of the favored treatment? When they didn't, Joseph must have breathed a sigh of relief.

The Final Test

But Joseph wasn't finished testing them. When he sent them on their way the next day, he told his steward to fill the sacks with as much food as the brothers could carry. Then, he said, put each man's silver back in the sack. And he told the steward to put his own silver cup into Benjamin's sack. No sooner had his brothers left than Joseph sent his steward in hot pursuit. Catching up with them, he accused them of repaying hospitality with robbery. The brothers, stunned, vehemently denied the accusation.

When they challenged the steward to open any of the sacks, they were shocked to find the silver. And much to their chagrin, there in Benjamin's sack was Joseph's silver chalice. They had sworn it wouldn't be in any of their bags. If so, they had promised, the guilty party would return as Joseph's slave. Can you imagine how their hearts plummeted when the steward pulled the cup out of Benjamin's sack? What would their father do? Truly, it seemed as though their lives were unraveling.

Upon returning to the city, they were ushered into an audience with Joseph. Judah stepped forward to answer the accusations: "What can we say? How can we prove our innocence? God has uncovered your servants' guilt . . ." (Gen. 44:16). Once again these brothers acknowledged God's sovereign hand shaping and molding their circumstances. Judah gave an impassioned plea on Benjamin's behalf. He even offered to serve in slavery in Benjamin's place. The emotional impact pushed Joseph toward losing control. He sent everyone away—except his brothers. Pulling them around him, he said, *"I am Joseph!"* (Gen. 45:3, italics added).

Dealing with the Fallout

You can imagine the terrified silence of Joseph's brothers. The very air they were breathing caught in their throats as they stood on the edge of an emotional precipice and peered over it. Their hearts pounded. Their eyes burned. Their palms grew moist. Their legs felt like lead weights.

Joseph? Was it possible?

Pulling them even closer, Joseph set their minds at ease: "I am your brother Joseph, the one you sold into Egypt! And now, do not be distressed and do not be angry with yourselves for selling me here, because it was to save lives that God sent me ahead of you. For two years now there has been famine in the land, and for the next five years there will not be plowing and reaping. But God sent me ahead of you to preserve for you a remnant on earth and to save your lives by a great deliverance" (Gen. 45:4–7).

In his wisdom and grace, when he saw they were ready, Joseph greeted his brothers honestly and directly. He managed to shake the fear out of this reunion and replace it with joy. He effectually restored the relationship with his brothers—not by ignoring the past, but by acknowledging it and testifying to God's sovereignty in the midst of difficult circumstances. Most importantly, the confrontation had helped reestablish in his brother's lives a spiritual dimension as well as a relational dimension for living.

The Requirement of Repentance

Repentance, which leads to restoration, is the goal of legitimate confrontation. Joseph's brothers had to deal with their past. I suspect they had repeatedly thought about it but had regularly avoided it. Many of us do the same. We look for a more convenient season in which to repent of past wrong. We deny our guilt rather than dealing with it. We rationalize it away. Our fingers point in every direction, except back to ourselves.

At this point, though, Joseph's brothers stepped up and repented. In so doing they set an outstanding example for us all. Scripture, of course, is replete with the call to deal with our wrong. God says, "If you repent, I will restore you" (Jer. 15:19). He invites us to "repent and live!" (Ezek. 18:32).

But what does God mean when He says he requires repentance? Scripture teaches there is a true and a false repentance.

1. *False repentance.* I saw a lot of false repentance when I was at college. Many of the guys in my dorm would party all weekend. On Monday morning, when their heads felt as if they would explode, and their bodies would only move in slow motion, there was considerable "repentance." But it had no lasting impact. The next weekend they would repeat what they had repented of the previous Monday.

2. *True repentance.* Scripture says, "Godly sorrow brings repentance that leads to salvation and leaves no regret, but worldly sorrow brings death" (2 Cor. 7:10). Sorrow that is only skin deep won't change a person's life. It's centered more on the consequences than on the act itself. Godly sorrow, on the other hand, begins in the innermost part of one's heart. It causes us to mourn the wrong itself and not merely the consequences. It brings us face-to-face with the fact that we have broken God's heart. True repentance requires change. It also requires that wrongs must be corrected and relationships restored. Godly sorrow brings remorse because it recognizes that, ultimately, God has been offended by our behavior and our attitudes.

Joseph's loving but firm confrontation with his brothers yielded true repentance that could then proceed to restoration. Biblical confrontation grows from that goal. It always is based on a desire to strengthen those involved. Howard Clinebell, a well-known counselor, has indicated that confrontation combined with caring brings growth, just as surely as judgment and grace lead to salvation.

That's Great for Joseph, but . . .

Hardly anyone really likes to be on either end of confrontation. We'd prefer it if there were a Plan B. I'm sure

Joseph was no exception. He probably would have liked to have moved immediately to forgiveness and restoration, if that were possible. But it wasn't.

We noted in the previous chapter that forgiveness is a hallmark of healthy relationships. It protects relationships that are still relatively sound, and it restores those that have been torn apart by adversity. Forgiveness enables us all to get along, something obviously important to our Lord Jesus Christ. After all, in His prayer in Gethsemane, He said His deepest desire was to see His followers living in unity (John 17). Other Scriptural injunctions clearly require us to strive to "live at peace with everyone" (Rom. 12:18). So shouldn't we just keep quiet and continue "turning the other cheek"? Shouldn't we be forgiving rather than confronting?

Sometimes . . . but the balance of Scripture indicates that confrontation is sometimes necessary, and it spells out the correct way to handle it. We have, of course, Joseph's example. But there are many other examples as well, including Jesus Himself, Who confronted His disciples numerous times because of their lack of faith. He challenged the money changers and drove them from the temple because of their incorrect actions and attitudes. He confronted Martha when she was so busy doing things *for* the Savior that she wasn't taking time to be *with* the Savior.

The ability to handle confrontation in a positive manner is a requirement for living life to its fullest, for true unity often cannot be achieved without some level of discussion which leads to eventual agreement. Therefore, it's crucial that when confrontation is required, it must be done correctly. Whether it happens at home with a family member, at the workplace, in the church, or between friends or acquaintances, the principles for loving and successful confrontation remain the same.

Examine Yourself

Tough love doesn't begin with the actual confrontation—it begins with a self-examination. Jesus clearly told His followers, "Why do you look at the speck of sawdust in your brother's eye and pay no attention to the plank in your own eye? . . . You hypocrite, first take the plank out of your own eye, and then you will see clearly to remove the speck from your brother's eye" (Matt. 7:3, 5).

Many people have used this passage to imply that confrontation is never in order in the Christian life. In context, though, these verses follow instruction in the Sermon on the Mount where Jesus indicated that believers would have to make judgments that could lead to uncomfortable confrontation. Rather than eliminating confrontation as an option, this passage simply points out that effective confrontation begins with a detailed self-examination to make sure our own motives and behavior are above reproach.

Joseph had clearly accomplished this, for he had moved beyond the desire for revenge. He expressed no underlying bitterness or anger. His ultimate goal was restoration and reconciliation—himself with his brothers, and his brothers with their God.

As Joseph confronted his brothers, there was no demanding force in his actions. David Augsburger reminds us that "confrontation invites another to change but does not demand it."[2] Even God doesn't demand that we change our behavior—He invites it. And as we learn to imitate His example in all things, including confrontation, we will find that the only proper motive for this kind of action is to honor God, both in the way we handle the situation, and in the resulting restoration and reconciliation—person to person, or person to God.

Principles for Effective Confrontation

Once you have accomplished your personal inventory, and you are convinced that your motives and your behavior are pure, there are still some principles that will lead us through the actual process of confrontation.

1. *Overlook minor issues.* In every relationship, you will experience numerous irritations. Most of these are minor issues which should be overlooked. I don't mean you should allow the frustrations to build until they become major sore points. I mean you should put them aside mentally and emotionally and not allow them to create an open and infected relational wound.

2. *When sinful actions or attitudes are too serious to be overlooked, confront.* Consider the potential harm to the reputation or well-being of the other person. Remember that Scripture tells us, "Better is open rebuke / than hidden love. Wounds from a friend can be trusted . . ." (Prov. 27:5–6).

3. *Communicate how much you care about the other person.* You must genuinely consider how the confrontation will affect the other person. The old idiom says, "No one cares how much you know until they know how much you care." If possible, begin by stressing positive characteristics or actions before you begin the process of pinpointing the areas that require confrontation.

4. *Gently seek to facilitate repentance and restoration.* The apostle Paul gave instruction regarding confrontation

when he noted, "Brothers, if someone is caught in a sin, you who are spiritual should restore him *gently*" (Gal. 6:1, italics added). In this context, the careful choice of words and the tone of voice will make all the difference in the world.

5. *Choose an appropriate time and place.* This will be a judgment call. There is no perfect time or place. But a few guidelines can help. As often as possible, don't confront someone in the presence of others. Instead, look for a time when the discussion can occur in private. This avoids embarrassment that often leads to hostility. And do your best to find a time when outside pressures are reduced, and when circumstances will not bring up emotional baggage from other issues.

6. *Raise issues, not voices.* Stick to the facts, and don't get caught in emotional upheaval. Don't use phrases like "You make me . . ." Instead of placing the blame on the other person's shoulders, a better approach would be to say, "When this happened, I felt . . ." Too often emotions take control because we have saved a number of emotional IOUs. Rather than dealing with confrontation when the situations originally occur, we let them build. Molehills become mountains, and mountains become volcanoes. By sticking with the issues as unemotionally as possible, we don't bring in old baggage. We also don't bring in unrelated experiences or references. We deal with the issue at hand. We find the strength to attack the problem and not each other.

7. *Give specific examples of the wrong that is being addressed.* Avoid generalizations such as, "you *never* . . ." or "you *always* . . ." They are almost always gross exaggerations. It may even be helpful to write down the items you want to stress before you engage in discussion. Ken Sande,

an expert in confrontation and reconciliation, gives helpful guidelines to keep in mind when you write down thoughts before confrontation occurs. He suggests that you note:

- The issues that you believe need to be addressed. (Define the problem as narrowly as possible so you can focus on the central issues and not get distracted by minor details.)
- Words and topics that do not need to be included in your discussion and should be avoided because they are likely to offend the other person.
- Words that describe your feelings, for instance, *concerned, frustrated, confused, disappointed.*
- Description of the effect the problem is having on you and others.
- Your suggestions and preferences for a solution to the problem.
- The benefits that will be produced by cooperating to find a solution.[3]

Taking a few moments to collect your thoughts and structure them will help you avoid being drawn off into emotional minefields.

8. Strive to give the benefit of the doubt. Your goal is not to win—it's to resolve a conflict. You're not trying to prove the other person is drastically wrong while you are totally right. Give the other person the benefit of the doubt rather than declaring him or her guilty before you've even heard the other side of the story.

9. Avoid leading questions. Manipulating and demanding questions tend to stifle healthy confrontation. Don't begin questions with phrases like, "Wouldn't you say that . . ." or "Don't you feel that . . ." or "When are you finally going to do something about . . ." Inevitably the other party will respond with resistance and hostility. Remember, anger is a natural emotion, and it tends to surface at points of confrontation. It may provide a certain emotional release when expressed, but it usually ruptures relationships even further. Scripture gives wise counsel therefore when it says, "Everyone should be quick to listen, slow to speak and slow to become angry" (James 1:19).

10. Above all, pray. When you are forced to initiate or receive confrontation, bathe it in prayer from beginning to end. While there are no guarantees, the bottom line is that God can make an amazing difference when difficult issues arise. I recommend that you ask God to restore peace through the confrontation. Ask Him to give you a pleasant and positive countenance during the encounter. And thank Him—I know that sounds crazy—but thank Him for this opportunity in which both you and the one being confronted will grow.

Tough Love Works

One of my favorite books as an adolescent was Jack London's *White Fang*. White Fang was three-fourths wolf, an outstanding specimen of an animal. In his early years the law that guided his life was simple—survive at all costs. The men who controlled his life were vehicles of anger and hate. White Fang served them only out of fear for his life.

Then one day a kind man by the name of Wheedon Scott became his new master. He was different from the men White Fang had served previously. The love he exhibited reached deep into the heart of the animal and stirred the dormant dog nature.

With each passing day White Fang began to change. A new nature began to develop. Whereas his life to that point had been characterized by aggressive fighting, he now yearned to serve his new master. The transformation was beautifully portrayed when White Fang was confronted with a need for change. He had lived so long on the flesh of tender birds that he could not understand what was wrong with killing and eating chickens. Yet his new master confronted him with displeasure.

For White Fang it was a cuff on the ear—not a devastating blow, but one that indicated displeasure. It hurt his heart more than his body. But because the confrontation was done in love, he responded with change. He wanted more than anything to please his new master. Soon his behavior had changed so much that his master trusted him to sleep in the middle of the chicken yard. The love of his new master, even at the point of confrontation, changed White Fang's life.

It can be the same for you and me. If we deal with confrontation in the same way, our lives also will change. If we are being confronted, we must accept and seriously consider the criticism, and if necessary, we must recognize the need for change. Rather than resenting the challenge, we should be thankful for it.

And when we need to confront someone else, we should not avoid it, but approach it with care. Joseph confronted his brothers and caused them to reevaluate the vertical and horizontal dimensions of their lives. This confrontation changed them. It inevitably brought Joseph and his brothers closer together.

Confrontation does not have to be destructive. When used appropriately, it can instead be one of the most constructive actions imaginable.

Putting Yourself in the Refiner's Hands

1. Recall the five options we have in confrontation, according to David Augsburger. Which of those options most clearly characterizes your usual method of dealing with confrontation? List two specific ways that you can move toward more of a win-win posture.
2. Joseph confronted his brothers when it would have been easier either to avoid the situation altogether or to really let them have it. Summarize how he handled the situation.
3. In your own words, explain the difference between false and true repentance.
4. List the guidelines given in this chapter for effective confrontation. On a scale of 1 to 10, with 1 being poor and 10 being great, how do you match up to these ideals when you are involved in confrontation? What do you need to change so you can rate yourself as "10" for all of them?

TWELVE

A Lifetime of Refining for a Strength That Lasts

ART PEASE, A SPECIAL OLYMPICS RUNNER, decided in 1990 to enter a five-mile race scheduled in conjunction with the Portland, Oregon, marathon. Having run for three years in Special Olympics, he was eager to attempt this new challenge. In the confusion at the starting line, however, Pease inadvertently ended up with the runners who were competing in the normal 26-mile, 385-yard marathon. About an hour later, Pease realized something was wrong and that it seemed like "an extremely long race." But, undaunted, he finished the race as the only Special Olympian to run the full marathon. Asked why he continued to run once he realized the mistake, he simply replied, "I always finish what I start."

Art Pease intuitively knew something that many of us miss. Finishing is important. And I don't just mean in the physical sense of running a race. Billy Graham has shown that same determination in the race of life. On his seventieth birthday, *TIME* magazine wrote a significant article about him and his impact on the world. The end of the article noted that consistently this giant of the faith makes this request: "I pray that before I do anything to embarrass my Lord, He would take me home." The article then ended with the words, "So far, so good."

How You Finish Makes All the Difference

Throughout this book, we've seen that the refining process, as arduous and difficult as it may be, always begins with the end in mind. The process is not an end in itself—it's a means to an end, and that end is a useful product. The heat and pressure that form the ore into useful instruments are absolutely necessary.

Art Pease and Dr. Billy Graham both remind us that the same thing is true in life. The goal of refining is to shape and create an effectual tool for the Father to use in building His Kingdom. For most of us, that means the Master Refiner has a lot of work to do. He has to melt us and skim off the slag and mold us and shape us. The refining process is rarely a short-term project. Rather, it is a lifetime journey. He is consistently improving us. Cleansing us. Shaping us. Refining us. And He doesn't stop until He takes us home to stay forever in His glorious presence.

Joseph Finished Well

The last chapter of Genesis records Joseph's incredible ability to see that every event in his life—seemingly good or seemingly bad—was due to the refining hand of God. Regardless of what may have seemed difficult and hard to bear at the time, Joseph was able to look back and see God's sovereignty. Speaking to his brothers, he said that God had intended every experience "for good" (Gen. 50:20). A writer of the New Testament also tells us that, when the end of life was near for Joseph, he was still living by faith in the One who had called him (Heb. 11:22).

What was it about his life that enabled Joseph to finish so well? The word *mettle* comes to mind. Webster's dictionary describes it as "a quality of character or temperament, especially high quality of character." Interestingly, it comes from the same root as the word *metal*. Both character and metal need, and benefit from, refining. But what are the elements of this lifelong process?

The writer of Hebrews sums up the refining process, comparing it to a race. In chapter 11, he lists a host of biblical examples—people like Joseph, who have already finished their events successfully and are now sitting in the grandstands rooting for us. Then in chapter 12, he builds on that.

He says, "Therefore, since we are surrounded by such a great cloud of witnesses, let us throw off everything that hinders and the sin that so easily entangles, and let us run with perseverance the race marked out for us. Let us fix our eyes on Jesus, the author and perfecter of our faith, who for the joy set before him endured the cross, scorning its shame, and sat down at the right hand of the throne of God" (Heb. 12:1–2).

Let's look at the qualities he identifies in that passage.

Encouragement From the Right Crowd

In my school years I had the privilege of running track. Our coach had an interesting idiosyncrasy. Every team member was required to be in the stands before and after his event. He told us he didn't want us hanging around with our friends, standing in line at the Snack Shack, or flirting with girls. Instead, when we weren't competing, he wanted us in the stands cheering on our fellow teammates.

That's the picture painted by the writer of Hebrews. He reminds us of those who have already proven that it's possible to finish well. Now they've joined the crowd in a stadium, and they're cheering for you and me.

Joseph was familiar with some of the incredible finishers listed there. He could look at those who had preceded him. But we have an even longer list of people we can look to for encouragement when the going gets tough. History is filled with spiritual Olympians who cheer us on:

- Noah is there when we're called on to do something we've never done before.
- Abraham is there when we're called on to go some place we've never gone before.
- Moses is there when we're called on to risk like we've never risked before.
- David is there when we're called on to lead like we've never led before.
- Peter is there when we're called on to be bolder than we've ever been before.
- Paul is there when we're called on to have a passion like we've never had before
- And ultimately, Christ Himself is there when we're called on to be obedient more than we've ever been before.

At each new turn of the marathon of refinement, God has encouragement waiting.

Not Alone in the Process

The lifelong process of refining sometimes seems incredibly lonely. At times I've felt that I was the only one running the refining marathon. But the writer of Hebrews obviously knew that danger well. He offered encouragement by the simple words, "Let *us* . . ." Thank goodness he used the plural. Despite how we feel in those difficult times when we feel like a single iron atom in the Refiner's melting pot, God's Word assures you and me that we're *never* alone. Even if every other person in our lives abandons us in the hot coals, God will *never, ever, ever* leave us to endure the heat by ourselves.

While I've been writing this book, the 1999 U.S. Women's Soccer Team won the World Cup. Michelle Akers, one of the team's outstanding players, was named the best women's soccer player in the world in 1991. People marvel at her dexterity and athletic prowess on the field. But appearances don't always tell the whole story.

In 1993, Michelle collapsed on the field in the Olympics Sports Festival. Doctors were unable to find the cause of her problem, until they finally determined that she had contracted Chronic Fatigue Immune Dysfunction Syndrome. Her breathing becomes labored. Sometimes it's all she can do to get back to the locker room and change her clothes without dropping to the floor in utter exhaustion. Her extremities get shaky and her vision blurs. Pounding migraine headaches nearly incapacitate her for days. Insomnia makes the nights long, and the lack of sleep robs her of energy.

But Michelle knows she's not battling this alone. She relies on the truth expressed in Christ's statement to Paul, "My grace is sufficient for you, for my power is made perfect in weakness" (2 Cor. 12:9). And Paul continues, "That is why for Christ's sake, I delight in weaknesses . . . in hardships . . . in difficulties. . . . For when I am weak, then I am strong" (2 Cor. 12:10).

So God is with us in every hardship. But He also puts us in communities of faith, among people who go with us through life's fiery trials. Scripture constantly calls us to encourage one another, be kind to one another, love one another, forgive one another, strengthen one another, etc. By the repeated use of the term "one another," He lets us know that we need the help, support, and encouragement of others.

Several years ago I saw the perfect illustration of the type of "one-another-ness" that God wants to see in His children. It was a Special Olympics event. The race was the 100-yard dash. The contestants were young men and women with Downs syndrome. As the starter's gun fired, they all took off down their respective lanes, giving it everything they had. The crowds cheered. The contestants ran. And the atmosphere was charged.

Everything went fine until about the seventy-fifth yard marker. Suddenly, one of the runners fell into the cinders. It was amazing—every Downs syndrome runner stopped to help his fallen comrade. Then, putting their arms around each other's shoulders, they walked across the finish line together. What a picture of encouragement and support in the difficult challenges we face. Ecclesiastes 4:10 says it well, "If one falls down, his friend can help him up. But pity the man who falls and has no one to help him up!"

Get Rid of the Weight

We have seen that a key part of the refining process is the removal of impurities. In racing terminology, the writer of

Hebrews reiterates it like this: "Let us throw off everything that hinders and the sin that so easily entangles . . ."

The phrase "everything that hinders" refers to excess weight. No runner would expect to win a 100-meter dash with a fifty-pound pack on his back. In fact, a serious runner makes sure that even his or her clothing is extremely light and flexible. When the runner prepares to race, he strips off everything except light-weight running clothes. These offer a freedom of movement and allow him to carry as little weight as possible.

The writer of Hebrews reminds us that the same should be true in life. We have to throw off the proverbial fifty-pound backpack. And let's face it—this isn't necessarily limited to life's bad things. Good things can be just as heavy, if they are keeping us from what is best.

I noted in previous chapters that as I've been writing this book I've grappled with a spinal injury. It forced me to radically alter my work schedule. Doctors required me to stop going regularly to my office and to cease all travel (of which I do a great deal) for the recuperation period. They told me very bluntly that if I didn't comply, I would inevitably face critical surgery.

I chafed at the change. But, during that time, I evaluated my work schedule. I rediscovered that *busyness* is not necessarily *godliness*. Sometimes activity crowds out quiet, reflective time. I realized it was possible for the work of ministry around me to kill the work of God within me, when the two are out of balance. I was reminded that a former Ivy League university president said if he wasn't taking at least an hour each day to think creatively and to dream, he had stopped leading his school and was simply managing it. I found areas where I could help others grow, mature, and excel by delegating work to them. This relieved some of the weight of my responsibility, but it also catapulted others into new areas of growth and accomplishment.

I came face-to-face with my own need for a new perspective. It was during this time that a poem from an unknown author helped me see life from a different viewpoint:

> I counted dollars while God counted crosses.
> I counted gains while He counted losses.
> I counted my worth by things gained in store.
> He sized me up by the scars that I bore.
> I coveted honors and sought degrees.
> He wept as He counted the hours on my knees.
> I never knew until one day by the grave,
> How vain are the things that we spend life to save.

Set Aside Your Sin

The author of Hebrews goes on to say that we must set aside the sin which so easily trips us. Most of us make a major biblical error in dividing sins into two categories: "biggies" and "seemingly insignificant ones." Yet it is often the minutia that trips us and sends us cartwheeling down the track.

This principle was demonstrated several years ago when the space shuttle was grounded unexpectedly. It seems that 135 small holes were found in the external fuel tank insulation. Investigation revealed the cause of the holes to be a certain species of woodpecker called the Flicker. These birds had effectively grounded a billion-dollar wonder of modern engineering. Remember—little things matter.

Every sin, whether we gauge it to be big or little, has the potential to kill some part of us. Radio personality Paul Harvey illustrated this principle of sin's peril. He told of how

Eskimos in the far north often kill wolves. The Eskimo coats his knife blade with animal blood and allows it to freeze. He repeatedly adds layer upon layer, until the blade is completely concealed by frozen blood. Then the hunter drives it into the ice, with the hilt buried and the blade sticking up.

When the wolf catches the scent of the bloody knife, he finds it and begins to lick it. The taste of frozen blood makes him ravenous. He begins to lick faster and more vigorously. And somewhere in the licking, he fails to notice the razor-dash sting of the naked blade. He slits his own tongue, and never realizes that his insatiable desire is being satisfied by his *own* warm blood. His carnivorous appetite just craves more—so he licks more—until the dawn finds him lying dead in the snow.

The human appetite for sin carries the same type of consequence, for Scripture clearly tells us that "the wages of sin is death" (Rom. 6:23). It may or may not lead to physical death, but at the very least it will kill a part of you that God created for His glory. The writer of Hebrews reminds us that we can only escape that tragedy by an act of the will and a conscious decision that we will not give in to sin.

And when we do give in, it's essential that we repent and seek God's forgiveness. Just as the refining process draws off the dross at least every two hours, so God wants us to keep our accounts with Him, and with one another, short. When an element of impurity is brought to our minds in the form of attitude or action, God's wants us to confess, repent, and put the matter behind us.

The Course Before Us

In the refining process, it is the Refiner who knows each step that must be taken to insure an excellent product. The process is not left to chance. Even so, God has mapped out the process of refining in our lives. Each step is ordered by His sovereign oversight. The writer of Proverbs states, "In his heart a man plans his course, / but the LORD determines his steps" (16:9).

God Almighty, the great Refiner, has marked out the process he has for each of our lives to enable us to become a product fit for use in His hands. God has a specific, strategic, sequential plan to refine your life and bring you to a place of fulfillment!

But beware of those who tell you it's going to be an easy journey.

In my junior year of high school, when football season came around, I was talking to some of my friends who were going to be on the team. I mentioned that I would love to play football, and they immediately encouraged me to do so. I explained that I had never played organized tackle football, but they simply smiled, shrugged, and said, "Don't worry . . . it's easy."

Following their suggestion, I went to see the coach and reported for tryouts the next Monday. I was given a uniform in which to dress out and was told to hit the field. About midway through the practice, the coach put his arm around my shoulders and pointed to our All-State fullback. In a moment, the coach said, the team would run a play. My job was to keep that man from getting through the line. He patted my shoulder pads and said, "Good luck, boy." Then he walked away . . . quickly.

I remember when the ball was hiked, and the quarterback slammed it into the hands of that All-State fullback. He came running through the line, and there were two hits: he hit me, and I hit the ground. Suddenly the lights went out. I was knocked out cold. By the time I regained sensibilities, I realized that everything had gone dark. Frightened, I began to scream, "I can't see! I can't see!"

The trainer had reached me, and he said, "Shake your head, Reccord." I complied, but things remained dark, so I cried again, "I can't see! I've gone blind!" By that time the coach was at my side, yelling for me to shake my head again. Doing so, I saw a pinhole of light. Suddenly I cried, "Wait a minute, wait a minute. I think my sight is coming back. I see a little light."

"That's because you're looking through the ear hole of your helmet, son!" the coach cried. My friends had lied—football was anything but easy.

The lesson was short-lived. A few summers later, some friends were going waterskiing at a lake. Overhearing their plans, I made the passing comment that I wished I could water-ski. They invited me to go with them, but I quickly explained I had never been on skis in my life. Almost with planned harmony, they echoed, "Don't worry . . . it's easy."

They took me with them. They set me on a wooden dock. They pulled out a long rope with a wooden handle, and placed it in my hands. They explained that the rope was attached to the boat. When I was ready to ski, all I had to do was yell, "Hit it!" They said the boat would take off and would pull me right into the water. I'd be skiing in no time.

There were a number of things they didn't tell me! For instance, they never said that when I yelled, "Hit it!" the boat would take off at full throttle. They never said that when the line became taut, it would almost jerk my shoulders out of socket. Nor did they tell me about the splinters in the dock where I sat! But the thing that still bothers me to this day is that they never told me, "If you fall down, let go of the little wooden handle!"

Needless to say, my first attempts at skiing were a disaster. All because some people said, "It's easy . . ."

Nowhere in Scripture do I find the writers saying the Christian life and the refining process will be easy. It says we are to run "with endurance." That indicates that it will be something less than easy. In fact, we may find ourselves face down in the cinders on occasion. Biblical endurance requires us to stand back up, brush ourselves off, and get back in the race.

Several years ago, when Walter Payton played running back for the Chicago Bears, he was involved in a football game with the New York Giants. One of the announcers observed that, at that time, Payton had accumulated over nine miles in career rushing yardage. Without missing a beat, the other announcer remarked, "Yeah, and that's with someone knocking him down every 4.6 yards." Walter Payton, one of the most successful running backs of all time, knew that endurance is the only thing that gets a person to the goal. The key is not how many times you're knocked down—it's how many times you stand back up and start running again.

The Concentration Needed

The refiner knows the exact steps that will insure an outstanding, quality metal product. One set of procedures will produce a beautiful gold ring. An equally specific set of steps will produce a steel girder. Each process requires a refiner and forger who knows exactly what he's doing, and what product he's ultimately aiming to produce. It requires ultimate concentration.

In the same way, the writer of Hebrews reminds us that the race of life also requires focused diligence. When I ran track, my coach taught me important things about the value of concentration. I can still hear him saying,

- "When you run, don't look at your feet, or you'll trip and fall."
- "Don't look at the crowd, or you'll lose perspective of where you are."
- "Don't watch your competition, because it will distract you from your race."
- "As you run, keep your eye on the finish line and don't ever let it waver."

Our Hebrews passage echoes my coach's advice. It tells me, and you, to maintain our focus on the finish line. And since our ultimate goal is to be like Christ, it reminds us to concentrate on Jesus Christ Himself. He alone has run the race with perfection, showing us what a refined product of Christian faith looks like.

The secular world knows the power of focus. Think of Michael Jordan driving for a basket. Or Tiger Woods teeing off in a major tournament. Picture in your mind the 1999 U.S. Women's Soccer Team, consumed with the focus of winning the World Cup. Remember Lance Armstrong returning from a battle with cancer to win the Tour de France.

And there are Christian examples as well. David Livingstone set his eyes on the challenge of changing the world when he prayed, "Lord, take me anywhere, only go with me. Lay any burden on me, only sustain me. And sever any tie in my heart except the one that binds my heart to yours." And in our day, Mother Teresa certainly was focused on helping those in need who could not help themselves.

But Christ Himself is the preeminent example of focused concentration. He set His sites on a singular goal. He gave Himself as the ultimate sacrifice to provide the opportunity for you and for me to have a personal and intimate, growing relationship with God. It would take Him all the way to the cross, which He would endure because of the joy He knew would wait on the other side. And what joy was that? It was the joy of offering, once and for all, the access to a personal relationship with God. He did it for you and for me, and He didn't even let the shame and suffering of the cross distract Him from the ultimate goal.

How are you doing on keeping focused on the ultimate goal of becoming conformed to the image of Jesus Christ in your life? Are you becoming more like your heavenly Father every day? Are you willing to do whatever it takes to reach that goal? The refining process carries a large price tag—it demands surrender and sacrifice. You must surrender your will to God's, and be willing to sacrifice everything to finish well.

Cassie Bernall understood that.

On the morning of April 20, 1999, she was at Columbine High School in Littleton, Colorado, when explosions and gunshots shattered all vestiges of normalcy. Eric Harris and Dylan Klebold had launched a reign of terror on their classmates. Members of a disenfranchised group in the high school called the Trench Coat Mafia, they planned to wreak havoc on their school and then go out in a blaze of glory.

In the school library that morning, they faced seventeen-year-old Cassie and asked if she believed in God. When she answered without hesitation, "Yes, and you need to believe in Him too," they shot her to death.

Just a few days before that, Cassie had made a video in which she talked about how much she wanted to make a difference for Jesus Christ. She surrendered her will, allowing God to refine her in His fire, because above all things, she wanted to be a fitting instrument in His hands. She had been reading a book in which she had marked a passage by Martin Luther King Jr., which she hoped to share with her youth group at church that very week. It read, "No man is free if he fears death. But the minute you conquer the fear of death, at that moment you are free . . . I submit to you that if a man hasn't discovered something that he will die for, he isn't fit to live!"

Cassie never got to share that quote at a youth meeting. But her victorious spirit gave a global voice to the sentiment that it expressed. She focused her energy and attention on having a faith that would not falter . . . even in the fire. Jesus referred to that kind of focus when he said, "If anyone would come after me, he must deny himself and take up his cross and follow me" (Matt. 16:24). Dietrich Bonhoeffer put it into twentieth-century terms when he said, "When Christ calls a man, He bids him come and die." While he was not talking about physical death necessarily, he *was* talking about death to one's own agenda in order to focus on God's agenda. How are you doing in your concentration and focus? And what cost are you ultimately willing to pay in the refining process?

The Ultimate Completion

The writer of Hebrews says that Christ's focus and concentration enabled Him to live out commitment to the ultimate completion of His calling. Having died on the cross, yet risen from the grave, He "sat down at the right hand of the throne of God." The tense of the original language indicates that He "sat down at a point in time with an ongoing and continuing effect." When Christ did this, He established for all time His right-hand rule over all creation. He also became the one who is able to see us through every step of the refining process, so we might finish well and reach our ultimate end.

So the next time you're tempted to get up when the fire gets too hot . . . or falter before the finish . . . or throw in the towel when things get tough . . . just remember the sentiment expressed in this poem:

The Race

Defeat! He lay there silently, a tear dropped from his eye.
"There's no sense running anymore—three strikes,
  I'm out—why try?"
The will to rise had disappeared, all hope had fled away.
So far behind, so error prone, closer all the way.
"I've lost, so what's the use," he thought, "I'll live with my
  disgrace."
But then he thought about his dad who soon he'd have to face.
"Get up," an echo sounded low, "Get up and take your place.
You were not meant for failure here, so get up and win the race."

With borrowed will, "Get up," it said, "You haven't lost at all,
For winning is not more than this—to rise each time you fall."
So up he rose to win once more, and with a new commit,
He resolved that win or lose, at least he wouldn't quit.
So far behind the others now, the most he'd ever been,
Still he gave it all he had and ran as though to win.
Three times he'd fallen stumbling, three times he rose again,
Too far behind to hope to win, he still ran to the end.

They cheered the winning runner as he crossed, first place,
Head high and proud and happy; no falling, no disgrace.

But when the fallen youngster crossed the line, last place,
The crowd gave him the greater cheer for finishing the race.
And even though he came in last, with head bowed low,
unproud;
You would have thought he won the race, to listen to the
crowd.
And to his dad he sadly said, "I didn't do so well."
"To me, you won," his father said. "You rose each time you fell."

And now when things seem dark and hard and difficult to face,
The memory of that little boy helps me in my race.
For all of life is like that race, with ups and downs and all,
And all you have to do to win—is rise each time you fall.
"Quit! Give up, you're beaten," they still shout in my face.
But another voice within me says, "Get up and win that race."[1]

Putting Yourself in the Refiner's Hands

1. Why is it important to finish well?
2. List two people from Scripture who finished well.

   List two people from church history who finished well.

   List two people you knew personally who finished well.
3. What characteristics helped those people accomplish a good ending?
4. Re-read Hebrews 12:1–2, and then write it out in your own words.
5. Cassie Bernall found a quote by Martin Luther King Jr. that shaped her response when faced with the ultimate cost of following Christ. King said, "No man is free if he fears death. But the minute you conquer the fear of death, at that moment you are free . . . I submit to you that if a man hasn't discovered something that he will die for, he isn't fit to live!" Prayerfully consider that statement, and then answer this question: What are you willing to die for?

Notes

Chapter 1

1. This heroic story was first conveyed to me by my friend Pat MacMillan of Team Resources in his seminar on Team Development.

2. Ephesians 2:10 says, "We are God's workmanship, created in Christ Jesus to do good works, which God prepared in advance for us to do." The actual word for workmanship in the original language means "masterpiece."

Chapter 2

1. Harold Kushner, *When Bad Things Happen to Good People* (New York: Schocken, 1981), 65.
2. Jerry Bridges, *The Pursuit of Holiness* (Colorado Springs, Colo.: NavPress, 1978), 19.
3. A. W. Dewar, source information search unsuccessful.

Chapter 3

1. These facts are recorded in the National Transportation and Safety Board's Aircraft Accident Report, #NTSB-AAR-90/06, July 19, 1989.
2. Dr. Bernie Zilbergelt, *The Shrinking of America* (Boston, Mass.: Little, Brown and Company, 1983), 88.
3. Quoted by John Maxwell, *Your Attitude, Key to Success* (San Bernadino, Calif.: Here's Life Publishers, 1984), 41.
4. Dietrich Bonhoeffer, *Cost of Discipleship*, as quoted in *Shepherd's Notes Christian Classics* (Nashville, Tenn.: Broadman and Holman, 1998), 20.

Chapter 4

1. For example, Ephesians 4:31 tells us, "Get rid of all bitterness, rage and anger." And Hebrews 12:15 warns, "See to it that no one misses the grace of God and that no bitter root grows up to cause trouble and defile many."
2. Ron Lee Davis, *The Healing Choice* (Waco, Tex.: Word Publishers, 1986), 133–134.

Chapter 5

1. Richard Foster, from a talk given at a conference at Focus on the Family, Colorado Springs, Colorado, early 1990s.

Chapter 6

1. Scripture also adds, "Do not say, 'I'll pay you back for this wrong!' / Wait for the LORD, and he will deliver you." "Do not say, 'I'll do to him as he has done to me; / I'll pay that man back for what he did.'" "Do not repay anyone evil for evil. Be careful to do what is right in the eyes of everybody" (Prov. 20:22; 24:29; Rom. 12:17).

Chapter 9

1. Stephen Covey, *Principle-Centered Leadership* (New York: Simon & Schuster, 1990), 108.
2. Patrick Morley, *The Rest of Your Life* (Nashville, Tenn.: Thomas Nelson, 1992), 88.
3. Henry Blackaby, *The Man God Uses* (Nashville, Tenn.: LifeWay Press, 1998), 9.
4. Donald Seibert, *The Ethical Executive* (New York: Simon & Schuster, 1984), 37.
5. Peter Drucker, *Management Tasks, Responsibilities and Practices* (New York: Harper & Row, 1974), 462.
6. Quoted in Sherwood Wirt and Kerstin Beckstrom, *Topical Encyclopedia of Living Quotations* (Minneapolis, Minn.: Bethany House Publishers, 1982), 50.
7. Harold Myra, ed., *Leaders* (Waco, Tex.: Word Books, 1987), 51.
8. J. Kenneth Wishart, *Techniques of Leadership* (New York: Vantage Press, 1965), 66.

Chapter 10

1. David Augsburger, *Caring Enough to Forgive* (Ventura, Calif.: Regal Books, 1981), 15.
2. Frank S. Mead, ed., *The Encyclopedia of Religious Quotations* (Old Tappan, NJ: Fleming H. Revell, 1976), 225.
3. H. A. Ironside, *Illustrations of Bible Truth* (Chicago, Ill.: Moody, 1945), 67–69.
4. Augsburger, 67.
5. Tim Friend, "Stitches in Time," *USA Today*, August 10, 1992, Section D, 1–2.
6. If the person you need to forgive is unable to be contacted or has died, a helpful resource may be Dr. Charles Stanley's book, *Experiencing Forgiveness* (Thomas Nelson, 1996).

Chapter 11

1. Copyright 1989, Carol Joy Music\ASCAP (Admin. ICG)\Word Music\ASCAP. All rights reserved, used by permission.
2. David Augsburger, *Caring Enough to Confront* (Ventura, Calif.: Regal Publishers, 1973), 53.
3. Ken Sande, *The Peacemaker* (Grand Rapids, Mich.: Baker Books, 1991), 158–159.

Chapter 12

1. Author unknown, found in *Finishing Strong: Finding the Power to Go the Distance*, by Steve Farrar (Sisters, Ore.: Multnomah, 1995), 12.